RED HOUSE *[Fire! Fire!]*

a LORDSTREET LiME

by

Tony Hall

Cover graphic - Christopher Cozier
Cover design - Dexter Lewis
Project management - Naima Mohammed

Also by Tony Hall

Jean and Dinah...who have been locked away in a world famous calypso since 1956 speak their minds publicly.

RED HOUSE *[Fire! Fire!]*

meta-village theatre

Also included . . .

MUD !

a ritual in mud and percussion

****

Tony Hall

using the
JOUVAY POPULAR THEATRE PROCESS

****

a LORDSTREET LiME

First published by AuthorHouse 06/02/04

ISBN: 1-4184-7410-X (e-book)
ISBN: 1-4184-4248-8 (Paperback)

Library of Congress Control Number:
2003099839

Printed in the United States of America
Bloomington, IN

This book is printed on acid free paper.

In Memory of Beryl McBurnie and the Little Carib Company

...Fire is burning
Man pull your own weight...

Bob Marley

jouvay — a community awakening

Table of Contents

RED HOUSE [Fire! Fire!]................... 1

MUD!.................................... 135

RED HOUSE *[Fire! Fire!]*

FOR THE MEMORY OF ERROL HILL

. . . the future is no longer any place
to duck or to hide . . .

Leonard Cohen

ACKNOWLEDGEMENT

*This play owes a special debt to Michael
Anthony
because it draws openly on the extensive
research
he has published on the history of the city
of
Port of Spain.*

USING HISTORY IN DRAMA: A Programme Note

1. The Water Riots of 1903

On March 23, 1903, the Legislative Council met in the Red House in Port of Spain to discuss a proposed "Water Works Consolidation Ordinance" that would regulate and tax the use of water in the City of Port of Spain and its environs. Citizens who wished to witness the deliberations were required to obtain tickets. Angered by what they regarded as an illegal limit on their freedom, the Committee of the Ratepayers' Association presented themselves at the entrance of the Council Chamber and, refusing tickets, demanded entrance. At this time there was a crowd around the door of about one thousand persons: a large force of police were guarding the building outside, until a quarter to two p.m., when stone throwing into the Council Room commenced with great violence; this continued for about three quarters of an hour completely wrecking everything exposed and sweeping the Council Room from side to side and wounding many there present. At 2.30 the public building known as the Red House was torched in two or three places. The Riot Act was read twice from the gallery on each side of the building, and the police were ordered to fire; the mob was rapidly dispersed. About this time a large force was landed from H.M.S. "Pallas", and a contingent of the local forces arrived on the scene. All efforts failed to save the Red House, which was completely destroyed with all records, except those in the Registrar-general's vault. The casualties from the firing were 16 killed and 45 wounded.

The 1903 riot in which the Red House was burned to the ground constitutes an important chapter in the history of Trinidad and Tobago. The nominal issue – water rates – was little more than a mask for a drama that involved race and class in a struggle for self-determination. The Ratepayers' Association was founded in 1901 by prominent citizens of Port of Spain, including Emmanuel "Mzumbo" Lazare, a leading member of the Pan-African Association. The Association resisted the imposition of an ordinance that would in their opinion deprive the citizens of Port of Spain an effective voice in their own governance. Though the Ratepayers' Association, which precipitated the riot, was largely a middle class association, most of those who were wounded or killed in the riot when the police were ordered to open fire were working class labourers, women, and even children.

2. Red House [*Fire!* *Fire!*]

The play depicts the events of this disastrous riot. Each of the characters portrayed is taken from history. Mzumbo Lazare, a great orator who held a military commission, was both a politician and a lawyer. A man of imposing personal presence, Lazare was an active reformer, a fighter for racial equality, who was at the same time respected and received in the highest circles of Port of Spain society. Sir Henry Albert Alcazar, the Mayor of Port of Spain for two years in the 1890's was also a lawyer who worked for reform. These two men were members of the Ratepayers' Society – middle class reformers who made it their business to fight for equality in a climate of colonial racism.

Other historical characters in Red House include: Captain Walter Darwent, the Fire Chief, whose delay in answering the fire alarm was a factor in the burning of the Red House; Sergeant Tom Holder, a policeman who used the occasion of the riot to get even with his estranged girlfriend Eva Carvalho. Finding Eva in Brunswick Square (now Woodford Square), Holder shot her at point blank range. Thus, sexual jealousy was satisfied under the cover of political action.

Though the events in the daily lives of these characters are heightened and dramatically coloured, the stories themselves are grounded in historical fact. The purpose of presenting them in 1999 is not, however, simply to re-create history under the stars. It is said that those who fail to learn from history are doomed to repeat it. The issues of equality, justice, racial integrity, and self-determination that fueled the riots in 1903 burn as brightly now as then, compounded by the spectres of vagrancy and homelessness that characterise our world today.

The Jouvay [Popular] Theatre Process asks actors to find in the characters they portray, the imps, robbers, jab jabs and other archetypes of resistance and affirmation that are at the heart of the Jouvay tradition. In this play this process has been woven through the historical drama, instilling a sense of the recurrence of the struggles, challenges, defeats and triumphs that remain at the heart of Trinidad history, enlivening the stories of personal and communal emancipation that constitute the then and the now of our lives.

Dr. Milla Cozart Riggio: Professor of English Literature
Trinity College, Hartford, CT

Compiled for the programme of the first production and based on research done at the Trinidad & Tobago Heritage Library through the kind courtesy of Pearl Eintou Springer.

CHARACTERS

Tourist Annie/Annette Sylvester
Narrator/Visionary/Dancer plays
Fat Lady (vendor)

**Ram, The Silent God/Manohar [Rachichacha]
Dookie**
Ex-agriculturalist & Drug Mule

Father/"Syrian"
Ex-priest & teacher plays
Capt. Walter Darwent (Fire Chief)
and *Alcazar* (lawyer/politician)

Sydney Fletcher
Ex-policeman plays
Sargeant Tom Holder (policeman)

Christina La Croix
Dancer/artist plays
Eva Carvalho (washerwoman)

Ricky Stewart
Ex-lawyer/poet plays
Mzumbo Lazare (lawyer/politician)

Lester Joseph [Joe Magic Machine] McLean
Ex-businessman plays
Greasy Pole (Man Around Town)

The first production of **Red House [*Fire! Fire!*]** by Tony Hall and Lordstreet Theatre Company was presented by the Baggasse Company in collaboration with The Normandie Hotel and Restaurant. The production was staged Under The Trees Normandie, St. Ann's, Trinidad & Tobago from March 10th to 21st, 1999.

The cast was as follows:

Noel Blandin	Sydney Fletcher/Sergeant Tom Holder
Wendell Etienne	Ricky Stewart/Mzumbo Lazare
Kenwyn Felix	Lester Joseph [Joe Magic Machine] McClean/Greasy Pole
Arnold Goindan	Manohar[Rachichacha]Dookie Ram, the Silent God]
Deborah Maillard	Annette Sylvester [Tourist Annie]
Christopher Pinheiro	Father [Syrian] Alcazar/Captain Darwent
Penelope Spencer	Christina La Croix/Eva Carvalho

Producer (The Baggasse Company)
Christine Johnston

Director
Tony Hall

Choreography
Stephen Hankey

Dramaturge
Milla Cozart Riggio

Music
Calliston Pantor

Set Design
Christopher Cozier

Costume Design
Meryl Mahabir

Properties/Specials
Lari Richardson

Lighting Design
Knolly Whiskey

Costume Construction
Margaret Sheppard

Stage Manager/Asst. to the director
Ken Joseph

Set Construction
Gary King

Production Manager
Trevor Jadunath

Scaffolding
Hi-Rise Limited

Executive Director (Lordstreet Theatre Company)
Naima Mohammed

RED HOUSE [*Fire! Fire!*] won four Cacique
Awards
for theatre in Trinidad & Tobago for 1999.

Most Outstanding Supporting Actor
Wendell Etienne
for Ricky Stewart & Mzumbo Lazare

Most Outstanding Supporting Actress
Penelope Spencer
for Christina La Croix & Eva Carvalho

Most Outstanding New Actor
Arnold Goindan
for Ram, The Silent God, Manohar
[Rachichacha] Dookie

Most Outstanding Lighting Design
Knolly Whiskey

Prologue: The Presentiment of Death

Act I: The Water Bill

Act II: Fire! Fire!

Act III: The Trial

Epilogue: The Funeral

Time: Monday March 23, 1903
and the same date in the present.

Place : The centre of Port of Spain
Republic of Trinidad & Tobago.

Prologue: The Presentiment of Death

(The stage is fully occupied by the burnt out structure of a large Victorian building. It is a replica of the Red House - the house of Parliament,

Port of Spain, Trinidad.

The façade on stage is a wooden frame that can be used in many different ways throughout the play. The actors must be able to scamper quickly up and down this frame and move about on it freely. There is a downstage playing area in front of the structure.)

Dawn.

Up stage right, high up on the wooden frame of the set, there is a silhouette of a man in a fireman's hat who appears to be riding a horse. We can only see him from his waist up. A part of the frame blocks the rest of his body. As he bobs up and down, we hear sounds of two people having sexual intercourse. This grows to a loud chorus. As they scream out their climax, the figure in the fireman's hat drops from sight.

A barefoot woman in a red dress (a

dancer), runs on stage from stage right. As she reaches centre stage a long bayonet emanating from stage left suddenly stops her in her tracks. She turns and looks back in the direction from which she came. There is no one there.

Stillness.

As she turns back to face the bayonet she is stabbed between the ribs. The bayonet retreats. At the same time a 12-foot tall apparition of the woman appears.

A presentiment of death. In a split second she sees it, screams and falls to the ground in a pool of red. Her red dress gathers around her.

Throughout this sequence the light of the day has been coming up so that by this time it is morning.

Enter TOURIST ANNIE. The apparition disappears.

(TOURIST ANNIE is a middle-aged woman of a racial mix commonly found in Trinidad. She is probably of Aboriginal, African, Indian, Chinese and European ancestry.)

TOURIST ANNIE

(to the crumpled figure on stage)
Get up, Christina, get up darling. Get up.

Yes. Oh Lord! Is out here you sleep last
night, girl? What happen? They take your
space again? Yes, dear. Go. Is almost
time to prepare yourself. (*Pause*).

*(Christina gets up drowsily and makes her
way off stage)*

We will have plenty people out here today.
*(Tourist Annie sets up a big iron pot on
two bricks, down stage right. Written on
the pot are the words:*
POT OF GOLD, Give to Receive.*)*

*(Enter Ram. He is a small Indian man, not
very old, perhaps in his forties. He comes
out dressed in an old pair of pants cut off
at the knees.
He is brushing his teeth vigorously.)*

TOURIST ANNIE

Not here. Not here, man. People coming
just now.

RAM

(still brushing his teeth)
Whag…yondoaun…kwanfug..yon…elf.

TOURIST ANNIE

Too much talk. Go and get yourself ready
somewhere else. *(Ram exits hurriedly. She
shouts after him.)*
And don't forget the banners…and the signs!
(She unfolds a large banner with a local

beer company's logo painted in bright,
colorful letters.
The banner reads:

THE LITTLE THEATRE
presents
THE WATER RIOTS OF 1903

(Enter a man dressed as a Roman Catholic priest while she is unfolding the banner.)
Morning, Father.

FATHER

(Irish accent)
Top of the morning to you, my lass.

TOURIST ANNIE

Yes. Yes. Come on, help meh with this thing.
(They put up the banner across the barricade.)

FATHER

We had a lovely service in the cathedral this morning. I haven't seen you at confession...

TOURIST ANNIE

Yes, yes. Go and get ready. We have a big day ahead of us. Don't forget all your things. The hat, your horse, the whip. You know you...Get something to eat before you come back. Ah put some food back there

for all yuh.
(Father exits)

FLETCHER *(off stage)*

Well then, where were you?

CHRISTINA

(Reversing onto the stage, visibly upset)
Why do I have to answer to you?
*(Father appears up stage in the frame of
the building.)*

TOURIST ANNIE

Fletcher, Fletcher, ease off!   All right?
Leave it alone!

(Enter FLETCHER.)

FATHER *(on the barricade)*

Children, children...

FLETCHER

(to FATHER)   Shut up, you 'Syrian Buller'!
(to TOURIST ANNIE)   Did you know that she
was not in here last night?

TOURIST ANNIE

Yes! *(Pause)* *(Christina leaves the stage)*
  (FLETCHER looks up at FATHER.   FATHER

disappears.)
Leave her alone. *(pause)*

FLETCHER

Look, I don't think this thing is a good idea. And with all them tourists who come down here these days...I have word from the Council men that if we go ahead with this 'riot' today, it could cause real trouble.

TOURIST ANNIE

For whom?

FLETCHER

The police say they done warn us already and that is more than they were prepared to do in the first place. *(TOURIST ANNIE ignores him. She picks up a bell that was nearby and rings it vigorously.)*

(Enter STEWART, a sturdy man of African ancestry wearing a pair of old sneakers on his feet, a small trinket-sized tenor pan hung around his neck and a gold crown on his head. He jogs backwards across the stage. He is carrying a full brown paper bag under his arm.)

STEWART

Beware the twenty-third of March. Beware...
(JOE MAGIC MACHINE appears up on the frame.)

JOE

Hail, the King! From the House of Stewart…
*(STEWART flings the bag and its contents in
the direction of JOE and exits.)*

TOURIST ANNIE

Magic Machine! *(JOE disappears)* Go and
get ready. Is almost time … Look, people
gathering already. Go on. *(FLETCHER
exits, she rings the bell some more)*.

FADE

End of Prologue

ACT I: THE WATER BILL

Enter TOURIST ANNIE. *(There is a fanfare of percussion to announce her entrance.)*

The occupants of this space spend a lot of time beating out percussive rhythms. They use sticks, pots and pans, anything found in the rubble of the burnt out building they now occupy. They beat on their bodies, to ease their pain. They even sometimes hum for relief or jump up and down on the spot. There is the odd, old tenor pan hanging around.

TOURIST ANNIE is dressed in a huge colourful skirt. It flares out from the waist and goes down to the ground. It is fitted with tambourines and metal cymbals that she can play from time to time. It is a celebration skirt with the Dame Lorraine treatment. On her feet, ankles and wrists are fitted bells, which she uses to good effect when she moves or dances. On her head she wears a majestic wrap which gives her an extra foot or so of height.

She enters and ritualistically covers the four corners of the space as she periodically taps out a rhythm on her 'drums'. She is in full command. She begins to play for an audience of tourists.)

TOURIST ANNIE

Hello darling, lovely day isn't it? Yes…
I am called Tourist Annie. Welcome, to my
islands, these islands of paradise. Every
man is an island in this Caribbean, from
Caliban to Friday, from Columbus to Castro
(*Pause*).

I know you do not know the history. The
history of my people. So let me tell you.
The Little Theatre's play for today is
called THE WATER RIOTS OF 1903.

Ram, The Silent God, alias Manohar Dookie,
also known as Rachichacha, will play an
Indian, man. Take a bow Ram, quickly,
quickly, come on. Next Father Elias, whom
we, affectionately call "Syrian", plays
Captain Walter Darwent, the Fire Chief and
he also plays Henry A. Alcazar, a lawyer
and politician. Hurry up nah man. Yes,
Sydney, Sydney Fletcher plays Sargeant
Tom Holder, a policeman. Christina La
Croix plays Eva Carvalho, a well-known and
popular washerwoman. Oh God, all you hurry
up nah man. Come Ricky, Ricky Stewart,
ladies and gentlemen. He plays, a man of
African stock, Mzumbo Lazare, influential
lawyer and politician. Lester Joseph McLean
alias Joe Magic Machine plays Greasy Pole,
man around town. Bow. Bow, nah you.

Ok! So, we ready. As the story goes, it
all happened on this very spot years ago,
many, many years ago today. So this is an

anniversary.
(*Applause from the players backstage*).

Ram, the first placard. Come! Come! *(Ram
eagerly walks around the stage with a
placard, which reads*:
"The Walsh Wrightson Water Bill".)
Good, we begin. The Walsh Wrightson Water
Bill.
*(A small crowd follows him on, carrying
mainly placards, red flags and banners, one
of which reads:*

**Let Mzumbo Lazare Speak!
The Ratepayers Association**

*(RICK STEWART as MZUMBO LAZARE climbs the
barricades of the building to loud cheers
and applause.*

*MZUMBO is dressed in a collar and tie. He
is a well-known solicitor.*

*TOURIST ANNIE sits on a stool downstage,
near to the* **POT OF GOLD***, and looks at the
action.)*

MZUMBO

Citizens, we have a problem. A serious
problem. Coming down the road just now,
through that big-shot area of St. Claire,
I see taps running, running. Those taps
are running habitually. And yet these
people claim inadequate water supply? As
you know they have their large plunge baths
and sometimes they take all day to full.

27

Yes, as much as 2,000 gallons, some of them. Now Mr. Wrightson, that honourable gentleman, the Director of Public Works, two years ago forced the enforcement of the law to cut off people pipes clean, clean. Anytime he find your pipes have runnings or they in disrepair, he coming to cut. In 1901, just two years ago, he cut off 185 pipes. I have it here. *(He holds up a document).* Look, for the first eight weeks of this year he cut 181 already and most of them without any notice to the people. It is true that this cutting and cutting has allowed a small supply to go to that outlying village Woodbrook. But, I am afraid, there will be a serious shortage in a few months, for the problem is wastage and poor supply. Instead of dealing with that they are going to force us to pay hellish high rates while those people up there continue to waste what little we have. The issue is water. And water is the staff of life. We have to be warriors for the rights of the people. *(Half-hearted cheers) (FLETCHER breaks from the crowd and moves downstage to TOURIST ANNIE).*

FLETCHER

Look, Annie we cannot go through with this.

TOURIST ANNIE

Fletcher! This is not a rehearsal. This is the real thing. We are in it already.

MZUMBO *(continues on the barricade)*

The government never gives you full information on the water works scheme. And nobody is really thinking of alternative schemes for water supply. Governor Alfred Maloney and his Legislative Councilmen do not care one hoot about any of us. Who represents you on that council, eh? Tell me. Who are these councilmen? Remember it was in 1889 that the Borough Council was abolished. There and only there we had elected representation. I made a demand for its restoration. But what? I say it to you now, loud and clear. And I don't care who hears. The interests of this government are not the interests of the people. But remember this is one of His Majesty's most important and prosperous colonies and as I said to Her Royal Highness Queen Victoria at her Jubilee some years ago: "Madam, in Trinidad we are all English". And she said: "But sir, it is said that you, Mzumbo Lazare, are of pure African stock ", and I replied, "Yes, your Highness, but I am still English". *(Loud cheers)*

JOE

(Downstage to TOURIST ANNIE)
Annie, I have to talk to you.

TOURIST ANNIE

Not now, Magic. What is this? The play has started. People are here and they have paid good money.

JOE

I know, I know. But Fletcher is up to
something. I don't like it

TOURIST ANNIE

Yes. Yes. The Councilmen have warned us
many times about this site. *(To their
audience).* Look, we are doing our work and
they are doing theirs. We have made the
place safe for you people, right? Right!?
(She gets a response from the audience.)

JOE

But he is saying that they have sold this
site and that is why we have to vacate it.

TOURIST ANNIE

Sold this site? Not that old talk again?
To whom this time?

JOE

I am not sure. I will find out.

TOURIST ANNIE

Okay, see what you can do. But not now.
Let's get back to the 'riot'. Please!
*(JOE goes back to the barricades. TOURIST
ANNIE turns to her audience)* And so the
Director of Public Works, Walsh Wrightson

was mandated by Governor Maloney and the rest of the Councilmen to frame a Water Works Bill to deal with the problem. This Bill, among other things, called for a special rate to be placed on large baths and the installation of meters.

CHRISTINA

(Downstage) Annie?

TOURIST ANNIE

Christina La Croix, what the hell you doing here? What is going on? This is the performance of a play of historical significance. We have an audience, and people willing to pay. What is going on today, lord?

CHRISTINA

I don't think this is a good idea. Fletcher... *(Fletcher comes downstage).*

TOURIST ANNIE

Yes, Fletcher...

CHRISTINA

There have been some exterminations carried out by the government already. My cousin was in the group that went the other night, from the old Trinity Cathedral site.
(Pause)

TOURIST ANNIE

This play has nothing to do with anything.
They don't care about this.
(*RAM stands by himself staring at them*).

FLETCHER

You really think so? Maybe when we first
started but look at the audience you have
now. You have to be careful.

TOURIST ANNIE

That is why they will leave us alone...They
can't afford to have the world...

FLECTHER

The Extermination Squad takes orders from
one man...

CHRISTINA

They make a real mess.

(*STEWART enters*)

TOURIST ANNIE

I know. (*pause*)

STEWART

We must stand our ground. We done take the
oath and swear together.

FLETCHER *(to STEWART)*

What oath, Tomboy?   You will take
responsibility?

TOURIST ANNIE

I am responsible.   *(pause)*   *(FATHER lights a
cigarette)*

FLETCHER

I thought everybody who did that was dead
by now.

FATHER *(to FLETCHER)*

Nobody dies before their time, boy.

CHRISTINA

I think nothing dies.

STEWART

What a pessimistic thought.   *(FATHER blows
out smoke)*

FLETCHER

Hot air.

CHRISTINA

Transcendence.

STEWART

Like a good fart.   *(He farts)*

FATHER *(laughs)*

You dead or what?

STEWART

Maybe, maybe not.   *(They both laugh)*

FLETCHER

*(Looks up and sees RAM still standing alone
and holding a placard which reads:* **WE ARE
SMALL AND THE SKY IS LARGE)**
What he looking at? This man always
sneaking around. Silent, silent.

JOE

Leave him alone.   *(He reads)* "We are small
and the sky is large".
(Then he says in Hindi) Ram, the Silent
God.

FLETCHER

Silent God, my arse. The man name Monohar
Dookie. I know him as Rachichacha and he
use to plant garden, right? The problem
was we find out what was in his garden.
Silent God alright. He is a ex-Deputy
Attorney General who kill his wife dead,
with one chop of his human rights hand.

JOE

He tell yuh so, nuh?

FLETCHER

No. I know so, boy.

JOE

Sure! Sure! *(TOURIST ANNIE signals them to get back to the play.)*

MZUMBO

(He moves GREASY POLE & EVA, played by JOE & CHRISTINA, downstage left). Listen, if we do not get together and organise ourselves, they will continue to walk all over us. Eventually there will be no stopping them. They must not be able to ignore us.

EVA

What you suggest?

GREASY POLE

Yeah! A plan uncle, a plan.

EVA

You and your Ratepayers Association.

MZUMBO

Now we know that they intend to go ahead and pass this bill tomorrow. They also want to charge an entrance fee to the house.

EVA

To keep us out.

GREASY POLE *(Sarcastic voice)*
No! To keep us in.

MZUMBO

Remember the last time we caused them real
trouble in the house with our numbers?
Edgar was disappointed and expected more
but at least we were able to delay them a
bit.

GREASY POLE

They trying to prevent that.

MZUMBO

Yes.

EVA

Isn't that illegal though?

GREASY POLE

What?

MZUMBO

The present system of legislation does not
allow for any consultation with the public
or anybody else for that matter.

EVA

So basically these people can do what they
want. (*Pause*). It is not fair.

GREASY POLE

What is fair?

EVA

I don't know. I don't know.

GREASY POLE

I have to meet a man out of town, in St.
Joseph. (*Turns to leave*)

MZUMBO

Greasy Pole…

GREASY POLE

Yes!

MZUMBO

All our people must come down here,
tomorrow. See what you can organise.
(*Pause*) We must show defiance. (*Greasy
Pole stops and stares at him*). All within
the law, law and order. You understand?

GREASY POLE

Sure, sure. (*He exits*)

EVA

What can we do, uncle?

MZUMBO

Is fire next time Eva. (*Pause*) You and the fire chief. Captain Darwent, friendly, yes?

EVA

Why? (*Pause*) I wash his clothes.

MZUMBO

You have clothes for him now?

EVA (*Quizzically*)

Yes. (*Pause*) Tomorrow he will come by me. (*Pause*) (*Up on the barricades the Ratepayers Association meeting is still in progress. Flags, banners etc... GREASY POLE is seen, busy, organising...loud cheers. Enter MZUMBO*).

MZUMBO (*On the barricades*)

It is good you have come out in your thousands. We have to show these councilmen tomorrow that we will not be anybody's fool. We will never be anybody's fool again. Let me tell you. It was Friday August 1st, 1838 that over 800,000 of us achieved emancipation. And now, today, they want to come up with an entrance fee to get into the house. But this is our house. The house of our business. Are we citizens? Or are we not citizens? This is no longer a decision for them to make. They cannot put us out. I say they cannot put us out. Ladies and gentlemen of the Ratepayers Association, have no fear. We have some friends in the council, people like the Most Honourable Henry Alcazar. They understand that this ticket business to get into our own house is illegal. Must be illegal. But you must understand that this came about because, by our presence, we stopped the hasty second reading of the Water Works Ordinance a week ago, on the 16th.

VOICE IN THE CROWD

But on the 23rd of March…!

MZUMBO

Yes! Friends, citizens, tomorrow Monday 23rd of March we know what we have to do.

VOICE IN THE CROWD

That day is coming!

MZUMBO

Yes, friends! The day is coming in this colony when we must take our rightful place in the house. In that house. The house of the father. We will not be homeless…And on that day…we will not be homeless.

VOICES

Homeless…homeless…

*While this chorus is being sung, Sargeant
HOLDER (played by FLETCHER) and CAPT.
DARWENT (played by FATHER) move down stage
secretly away from the crowd.*

HOLDER

Colonel Brake and a few of his men intend
to sneak into the library chamber tonight.

DARWENT

Is that necessary?

HOLDER

There are rumours of trouble tomorrow.

DARWENT

I know, stirred by that Mumzumbo character
and his good friend Edgar Maresse-Smith.

HOLDER

Bush lawyers. *(The crowd chants 'homeless,
homeless')* There is a plot to disrupt the
proceedings of the Bill. *(Pause) (They
hear a noise)* Anyway, the Police Chief
and a few members of the constabulary will
be in the house from tonight. *(The noise
again) (DARWENT moves and drags RAM, with
a small cart of goods, out of the shadows)*
Oh, it is the Hindu. He is always sneaking

40

around in silence. What did he hear? How
long was he there?

DARWENT

I don't think he heard anything.

HOLDER

He is not deaf. What did you hear? *(Pause)*
(Slaps him) Speak up, man.

RAM

Acha, sahib…Bas! No Bas! No Bas!

HOLDER

(Holds on to RAM)
English, English, man…

DARWENT

But you know that he speaks no English.

HOLDER

He should. He and his damn Hindustani.
(Lets him go) Hedon!

DARWENT

Run along. Run along, now. *(RAM exits)*

HOLDER

No! Don't let him go. We don't know what
he knows.

DARWENT

What do you suggest we do with him? *(Pause)* Look, as Fire Chief I can have the Fire Brigade on 'stand by' from early in the morning.

Holder

I don't think that will be absolutely necessary. We can handle this one. *(Enter GREASY POLE, he is sneaking around)* There is that good-for-nothing jailbird, Greasy Pole.

GREASY POLE

There is something I need to discuss with you Captain…Darwent…

HOLDER

Well, I will leave you two 'gentlemen' to it.

DARWENT

Okay Sergeant. *(Holder moves to exit)* Yes Mr. Greasy Pole.

GREASY POLE

Sir, it is a message from Miss Eva Carvalho. *(HOLDER slows down to listen)* She say she need yuh to pick up yuh clothes, for sure, tomorrow morning. *(Pause)* *(HOLDER exits)* She really wants to see you.

DARWENT

Oh.   Thank you.   Thank you.   Mr. Pole.
(Exit)   (More crowd chants)

*White Christmas tree lights define a pyramid
out of the structure on stage.   FLETCHER
appears on stage dressed in a suit.   We
see his face and shoulders isolated by a
spotlight as if it were a close-up on a TV
show.*

FLETCHER

Hello.   Sydney Fletcher, here to tell
you about Operation Pyramids. Colonial
Logic Investments Limited, the number one
investment conglomerate in the Americas
is proud to embark on a new project geared
to bring even more pride and dignity
to everyone who lives on these islands.
Everyone whose ancestors were dragged up
on these beautiful shores.   That project
is Operation Pyramids.   Now these pyramids,
made of transparent tuff-bond plastic lego
blocks, will house our head offices and
administrative complexes as well as tombs,
vaults and other utility chambers.   This
old Red House site here is earmarked to
be our headquarters.   At present we are
negotiating in an attempt to expedite the
final financial arrangements for the purchase
of the site.

Operation Pyramids, based on the pyramids
created through the innate genius of our

African ancestors, the Egyptians, is part
of our neo-African vision for the New
World. Entrance to all our pyramids will
be through the tops of the buildings from
your personal aerocrafts. The base of the
structures will never touch the ground.
The pyramids will float on a cushion of
air. Your feet will never be on the
ground. At the moment we await the outcome
of the negotiations and we intend to begin
construction very soon, once we get the go-
ahead from our international partners. We,
of Colonial Logic, wish you the best and
look forward to continue serving you in the
future. Good night.

*TOURIST ANNIE enters as FAT LADY with a
basket on her head. She sells caramel,
toolum and sugar-cake. She is with EVA.
When FLECTHER sees them, he hides.*

FAT LADY

Toolum! Sugar Cake! Come and get your
sweetness and your cakes!!!

FLETCHER

Shit!

FAT LADY

(Looking in FLETCHER's direction)

Wait nuh, I thought I see Holder by that
corner. By Marine Square.

EVA

Who Holder?

FAT LADY

How you mean, who Holder? You don't know
Sergeant Holder?

EVA

If I don't know that beast? Tom Holder. I
use to live with him.

FAT LADY

Eh heh? You live with Holder? *(Pretending
she didn't know)*

EVA

Yes, some time ago and up to now he still
wouldn't let me rest. He will do anything
for them Englishmen. *(Movement in HOLDER's
direction)* Look! It look like he self.
The hog. We can't stay here nuh.

FAT LADY

Wait, child. *(She takes the basket off her
head and sets it down. She breathes a sigh
of relief)* So you is the Eva? *(She looks
EVA up and down)* Well, well.

EVA

What you really have in the basket? A
little rock…

FAT LADY

(Laughs) ... cake and so on.   Tools of the trade, girl.

EVA

You know, one time I remember seeing you by the Savannah when it take three policeman to carry you down.

FAT LADY

Yes! They did say how I pelt them with rock...cake. *(Contained laughter.   They stop in consternation as they see HOLDER beating severely, what looks like, a man, in a corner of the nearby building).*

EVA

You see.   They will always get people like him to do their dirty work.   Let us move on.   *(She helps FAT LADY with the basket to her head)*   He done threaten to blast off my head already.   That Satan.   *(They move on a little.)*

FAT LADY

Child, what you saying?

EVA

People like him will never understand.   We must fight.   This is our place.   How could we just sit down and take whatever they want to dish out?   *(Pause)*

46

FAT LADY

Eva? Darwent understands? *(Pause)* Don't answer. It ent none of my business. But…

EVA

But what? He was always against the Wrightson Waterworks Bill.

FAT LADY

You wash for him?

EVA

I wash for him.

FAT LADY

You know what people saying?

EVA

I know what people saying.

FAT LADY

Be careful, child. They hate him bad.

EVA

He awright. His heart in the right place. These people crazy.

TOURIST ANNIE

(Turns to the barricades)
Fletcher! Get out…

FLETCHER

I am not responsible for what happens here
today.
(He exits hurriedly and sheepishly)

TOURIST ANNIE moves to her corner.
CAPTAIN DARWENT rides up on his horse (A
burroquite) to see EVA. There is a long
pause as EVA is washing clothes and DARWENT
tries to keep his agitated horse still.

EVA

You come?

DARWENT

You sent for me.

EVA

You have something to get tomorrow.

DARWENT

Why can't I get it today?

EVA

I not ready yet.

DARWENT

Suppose I can't come? You know what day
tomorrow is?

EVA

What you think will happen? *(Pause)*

DARWENT

You know how I feel. The bill is unjust.
You cannot have one law for the big-shots
and another for the masses. It is wrong
and I told them that, in no uncertain
terms, years ago.

EVA

And that is why they treat you so...

DARWENT

Nothing will happen. When we do something
we do it good and proper.

EVA

Who we? You not even English.

DARWENT

I wasn't born in England. They still
regard me as English.

EVA

But they hate you.

DARWENT

I hate them, too. Look, I know some
people say that my reaction to this bill is

because…

EVA

…of me? I hear the talk too. They also say that I getting all my ideas on politics from you.

DARWENT

People will talk.

EVA

They forget who my uncle is. Look, you better pull out now. Police swarming this place and that tyrant Holder does still want to come and harass me.

DARWENT

I thought you had enough of him. *(Pause)* My wife will go back to England.

EVA

Captain Fire Brigade, you have to go. Come to the valley tomorrow. Thanks for everything. *(Pause)* I know you care. *(DARWENT hesitates and does not move. EVA moves to him.)* You must go. *(He turns and rides away. She stands and watches him)*

Lights up in TOURIST ANNIE's corner.

TOURIST ANNIE

Indeed, it is a question of the vote and
education. Mzumbo and others know that
people in England could vote for whomever
they wished for he said this to a crowd
a few nights ago. But education is not
available to everybody. And as Darwent
explained to Eva on many occasions, the
English do not want everybody to have
access to education unless there is a form
of education that can make colonials easier
to rule. Keep them proud to be subjects.
They will regret abolition and never want
to rule themselves.

*Lights up on the structure as FLETCHER
is surprised to see JOE in the building.
FLETCHER carries a bottle of rum with him.
He takes a swig from time to time.*

FLETCHER

What you doing out here?

JOE

I have my place. You have yours.

FLETCHER

You know there are plans for this site.
Big, big, men from the Council Chambers
talk to me and we still out here doing this
stupidness. When the Extermination Squad
come I will not be around.

JOE

Don't talk to me about no big, big, men,
you hear. I know all of them traitors.
When I was Managing Director of Industrial
Steel I hobnob with all of them. Now if
they want to get rid of us I must know
and I will not be in the group to be
terminated.

FLETCHER

That is what I am saying. I have word that
the Squad wants to hit today. They were at
the Cathedral the other night…

JOE

What they want to know?

FLETCHER

I don't know.

JOE

How you mean you don't know. Who you
talking to?

FLETCHER

Is not who I talking to. Is who talking to
me.

JOE

It have anything to do with the 'riots'

down here?

FLETCHER

Nah! That is just play. Though I think we
should not be doing that. We should just
leave.
*(Enter STEWART jogging backward,
exercising. He carries a brown paper bag.
He is fit, sweating)*

JOE

King Stewart!! You know was when he find his
wife swimming with a man, and the goldfish,
naked in his waterbed and that send him to
drive his Mercedes straight into a wall,
that he start running backwards. He 'fraid
he butt another wall head on.

STEWART

Oh contraire!

JOE

You know what I like about you. Is how
many times you walk into the sea with big,
heavy stones, in your pockets?

STEWART

On divers of occasions, my boy. Divers.

JOE

And they save you every time.

STEWART

From flying back to Africa. Ill fated
destiny.

JOE

I hear a rumour that you fly off a cliff up
at Toco, and plunge hundreds of feet down
into the fierce, swirling, jaws of the rocky
ocean below. People say you cannot die.

STEWART

You got that right. The African man…

JOE

Mind you, jumping off the cliff may be a
rumour too.

STEWART

We will never know. Will we?

JOE

I just love how you jog away from your
past life and never look forward. An ex-
minister of a ruling party who rise to the
top from the dregs of the slums and draft
a dragonish public order act. (*Pause*) And
then, everything from the law practice you
give the wife. I, just lost mine. But no,
you is man.

STEWART

Fight for what is right. Fight for what is important.

FLETCHER

But you know, we really don't know if is because of the horns you was getting or is because Lord Blackboard, the calpysonian, sing how he 'fraid you and make you loss the election, you does jog backwards. You know why this man does jog backwards?

JOE

Why?

STEWART

My Cree brethren, who have lived for centuries on the Canadian Prairies, have a folklore character called The Contrary. This fella does move backwards to show people their forward motion.… If any.

FLETCHER

(Sneezes) Eshu! What a fool. You blasted monkey. That is the most amount of horseshit I ever hear. Where you get that?

STEWART

That is the play.

FLETCHER

Play! Play! So wait nuh, anything people
tell you, you does just imitate? That was
your experience?

STEWART

This play is my life.

FLETCHER

And he and all still can't make up his mind
if he want to be a born again African or a
….

JOE

(Laughs) …born again Indian.

FLETCHER

Them so can't get me to repeat nothing they
say. *(Mocks STEWART)*. This play is my
life. Why you don't hush?……….Hush! Hush!

(Enter FATHER)

STEWART

Look, I don't intend to live out no post-
emancipation, post-colonialism, post-
independency history on this plantation. I
have a mission.

FLETCHER

Now what you talking about?

STEWART

I am not just another African-American
afterthought who, for years, was under
the commercial trademark "Negro" you know.
Scars and stripes forever? Huh! A real
destiny was ordained for me the day I set
foot out of Africa.

FATHER

Which is?

STEWART

To be the soul, salt…..sweat of a new
world.   *(Pause)*

FLETCHER

Right… (*RAM crosses with a placard which
reads:*
AFRICA HAS NO FUTURE)

STEWART

*(He pulls out a piece of silver paper from
his pocket and presses it against a comb
and plays it like a harmonica. He sings…)*
Well I'm singing the soca blues
Once again
I said ah singing calypso blues
In the rain
Cause my mama and papa
don't hear me no more
And these ass-holes around me
don't even know the score.

57

Red House [Fire! Fire!]

> (He vamps a solo on his paper and comb
>   instrument)   (Pause)

FATHER

Anybody have anything to eat?

JOE

What?   All the bread and wine all you thief
from the church finish?

STEWART

Cannibals!   The flesh and blood of Jesus
Christ.

FATHER

Anybody have anything to eat?

JOE

Go and ask your rich, thieving father.

FLETCHER

You Syrian Buller.

FATHER

This slavery shit is just an easy way out.
Don't give me that shit!   Don't try that!
Most of your families were never slaves.

JOE

Aye!! Aye!! Aye!! (He rushes FATHER.

STEWART has to hold back the over-excited
JOE.)   (Pause)

FATHER

My father, old Elias, land up here because
this was the end of the journey from Syria.
They went through Spain, France, the
islands. And he didn't want to go back on
the ship. So he decide to get off and find
something to do. Forty years later he send
money back to his little village for his
people to put electricity and running water
in their homes.

STEWART

Look. Is the African who had to fight for
the human space out here. From New Orleans
to Rio. Then for all like you so to move
in and occupy. Is the melanin factor, boy.
We work that out in a laboratory in Ghana
centuries ago, before all of this. Now,
all we want is reparation and compensation.

FLETCHER & FATHER

What?

STEWART

Like all you deaf. This space that you
living in come through the window pains of
blues dance and steel pan, mas and samba.

FLETCHER

Sambo, what is this about compensation?
Monkey-man!

STEWART

You want this bag of humanity and more
for nothing? We must have a life while
everybody else out here feting on we head.
Respect the melanin! That is what the
world 'fraid, you know. The melanin. The
Pope, the Queen, the U.S. President, all of
them know this. *(Pause)*

FATHER

When my father found out I wanted to be a
Roman Catholic priest, he went crazy. He
wanted to disown me. Strange because he
feel he is a strong Catholic. Anyway,
my mother couldn't stand the bacchanal.
Especially after the murder of my elder
brother Mario. They say it was drug-
related. I, myself, don't know for sure.
It was a money feud in one of our stores.
(pause) Ma died slowly. *(pause)* All my
younger brothers still call me a buller
to my face on the street. My father vowed
that his money would never go to his son,
the buller. He even went to the Archbishop
and insisted they throw me out of the
church. The Archbishop did not want to do
it, but with tears in his eyes, he said he
had to. A weak man. *(A slight pause)*.
The old man gives generously to the
building fund.

FLETCHER

These bullers always want to cry. I can't take this.

STEWART

Wait! Let father speak.

(Enter CHRISTINA)

FATHER

I was cut loose unto the streets. No one would have me. I didn't care anymore. But out here I meet people like Christina, King Stewart and Tourist Annie, good people. *(Pause)* So, I have a life.

(Enter TOURIST ANNIE in a rush)

FATHER

Anybody have anything to eat?

(CHRISTINA pulls out a loaf of dry bread and pinches off a piece. She feeds it to FATHER)

TOURIST ANNIE *(To FLETCHER)*

They had you on TV talking about pyramids?

FLETCHER

Me?

TOURIST ANNIE

Yes, You!

JOE

What going on?

TOURIST ANNIE

And you, you went talking to a man in St. Joseph?

JOE

No. It wasn't me. (*He looks at FLECTHER suspiciously*)

TOURIST ANNIE

Where is the Silent God?

JOE

Probably sleeping somewhere grinding down his teeth like a shoe heel.

FLETCHER (*to TOURIST ANNIE*)

If anything happens around here, I will hold you and Stewart personally responsible.

CHRISTINA

Fletcher? What is this talk I hear about building pyramid on this site?

FLETCHER

Woman! I know nothing about what you speak.
You so always ready to accuse me. Where is
Ram? Eh? I tell all of all you already,
to stay here and make this play ain't
making no sense. We all know that. We not
safe here. Everybody know that.

STEWART

This is our place. We fight for this space.
Yes! We safe like Selassie I briefcase…
with documents.

FLETCHER

What fool…?

STEWART

*(Pulls out an old tattered leather
briefcase)*
You have in here, a compass and a Solo
sweet drink, visas, cash and so on. When
Selassie came, years ago, and then just
left? Something was up. That didn't
happen so, you know…not just so…Plenty
people was confused. What? God come
black. *(Pause)*
Yes, we safe here. *(To FLETCHER)* But the
question is, are we safe with you?

FLETCHER

Boy I protect the best of them when I was
in the force. Is me who first move on the

Drug Lords and them. Nobody, especially the Council Men, didn't like me for that.

JOE

But the talk is you was the first Drug lord anyway.
(*FLETCHER who by this time is half-drunk goes to hit JOE with the rum bottle. Both STEWART and TOURIST ANNIE move to hold on to FLETCHER.*)

FLETCHER

Magic Machine, I will re-arrange your… You always spreading some bad rake about me. Crime fighting is an art, boy. An art. And I introduce that art to this place.

JOE

You sure right about that.
(*FLETCHER gets away from TOURIST ANNIE and STEWART and hits JOE a solid one with the bottle. JOE is thrown to the ground. He is caught unexpectedly. He bleeds from his head.*)

FATHER

Children, children.

FLETCHER

You shut your mouth, bumsee man.

TOURIST ANNIE

Everybody here!!! Shut up!! What the hell
going on here today? We have the play
ready and we all set to go. We have a
chance to make some money. But you all
insist on fighting down your own selves all
the time. People are willing to hear our
story. But no, we have to beat down, beat
down each other all the time. Fletcher
fighting Joe, Joe fighting Stewart, Stewart
fighting Ram, Ram fighting Father. And
Christina … Oh Shit Man!!!

JOE

I didn't do…

TOURIST ANNIE

Shut up!!! *(pause)* What are we doing here?
Why you here? *(To FLETCHER)* Why you don't
just go? *(To JOE)*

FLETCHER

We should all go. The Termination Squad
coming…

TOURIST ANNIE

Fletcher, you go! Why you don't go? If it
is the Squad you 'fraid eh! *(pause)* Can't
you see? We can achieve the peace that passes
all understanding. Out here we are removed
from what we know and can become blessed
personally. We can be responsible for others.

What evil do we have to fear? People from all
over the world come to us. Why?

CHRISTINA

But Annie...

TOURIST ANNIE

Shhhh! Quiet. *(Pause)* Listen to yourself...
(Long Pause)

*Off stage (sounds of someone being severely
beaten)*

VOICE 1

Look the traitor. Beat his arse.

VOICE 2

The Silent God. Talk now! You mule! The
Drug Lord got your tongue? Eh? *(laughter)*

VOICE 1

Nah! You don't double cross Indian people
boy. You don't inform on your family boy.
And we is family. You understand? Fa...
..ma.....lee!

*(RAM is thrown onto the downstage area like
a sack of flour. His cart, with placards
etc. for the play, are shoved on behind
him. He lets out a blood curdling scream.
Silence. The others run around from the
barricades to his assistance as we hear*

voices and shuffling of the persons who attacked RAM. CHRISTINA and TOURIST ANNIE move to take care of him. CHRISTINA sits next to his small body. She puts his head in her lap.)

RAM

Ugh!   Errs!

CHRISTINA

Shhhhh eh!   It's ok.   Quiet.   *(TOURIST ANNIE hands CHRISTINA a towel.   She dries his tears and soothes his wounds.)*
It is alright,man.   Shhhh.   We can hear you.   We hear you.   We hear you.   *(She looks up at TOURIST ANNIE and then to the others gathered around.   The last person she looks at is FLETCHER.   She fixes her stare on him.   The others turn to him.   They all stare at him.   He just stands there.   A dark cloud descends from overhead)*

(MZUMBO's voice emerges from the rubble.)

MZUMBO

Don't forget!   Tomorrow! Go to the Red House tomorrow! And let Wrightson and all of them know how you feel about this…Water Works Bill.   We must stop their dirty work. Now!

FADE
End of Act 1

ACT II: FIRE! FIRE!

Dawn breaks.

*The excitement of the day is in the air.
Different people cross the stage as though
they have appointments and going somewhere.
The bluish-pink clouds of the dawn hang
heavy with expectancy.*

*RAM, heavily bandaged, walks around very
slowly with a placard which reads:*

FIRE! FIRE! IN YUH WIRE

*STEWART is taking a bath in an old washtub
on the end of the downstage area. It is
like an old fountain pond removed from
an open public square nearby. He rubs
himself vigorously, with a long brush
and soap, as only a person who is very
conscious of cleanliness can. TOURIST
ANNIE with a large colourful scarf in her
hands, and CHRISTINA with a calinda stick,
are shadowing each other in a slow-motion
calinda (stickfight) routine. This is a
ritual of the sunrise. Meditation to start
the day. They do this in silence for a
while. STEWART is in the tub. (Silence).*

STEWART *(Sings)*

On the 23rd of March,
The 23rd of March,
I tell you already

69

Red House [Fire! Fire!]

Is you to catch
Is you to catch. Yeah! (*Repeat*)
Every man go have to sit, on his own
bottom.
On his own bottom. And burst his own fart.
And burst his own fart.
And don't ask where I get that.

*FATHER appears up on the barricades doing a
Gregorian chant. (Pause)*

FATHER

(Conducting an early morning mass)
Children, let us meditate on this brand
new day the Lord has given us. And think
of our Lord Jesus Christ, his head crowned
with thorns and preparing to die.

CHRISTINA & TOURIST ANNIE

BOIS!!! (*CHRISTINA falters as if hit*)

FATHER

With blood streaming down his face a
mournful Christ is dragged through the
streets of this Port of Spain on this day
of our Lord, the 23rd of March.

TOURIST ANNIE

(Moves to her downstage area)
All right, all right Father. Is time. Is
time. Done with the sermon and take your
place.

FATHER *(Whispers to himself)*

And nobody sees him. He is an outcast on the street. Oh Mary, Mother of God...

TOURIST ANNIE

Stewart, if you scrub any harder you will end up a white man.

STEWART

Honorary, my dear! Honorary in yuh... And that is my business anyway.

CHRISTINA

Don't forget. I need that tub later. And I need it clean. Without your holy water, OK?

STEWART

Okay! Okay!, nuh. This is not your tub.

CHRISTINA

I know that is the old pond from the fountain in the square. A public tub.

STEWART

And is I who drag it and install it here.

CHRISTINA

So what?

STEWART

So what? So what? *(Pause)* It is mines.
That is what.

TOURIST ANNIE

All you! Go now nuh! Ram, you too. Shit
man! *(CHRISTINA leaves the stage RAM
hurries off behind her with the placard.)*

TOURIST ANNIE *(To her audience)*

Well darling! Now it is all excitement
because today is the day when they say
The Water Works Ordinance will have its
final reading and it will be passed by the
Assembly. That august body. They going
ahead with their bill. Mr. Walsh Wrightson
and the others. Those honourable men.
Sargeant Tom Holder send out a rumour, that
before the debate, they going to lockup,
tight, tight, behind bars, all agitators.
Apparently, as the story goes, he say that
Mzumbo was number one. But, as far as we
know, they can't find Mzumbo. He too smart
for them. He in hiding. Eva and them had
a plan. However, we hear that they lock
up Greasy Pole. Colonel Hubert Brake and
the boys say, they find Greasy Pole trying
to break in the Chamber last night. Poor
Greasy didn't know that, not taking any
chances, they did full up the Chamber with
Police.

Now, everybody confused. What Greasy was

up to? Some say, he was trying to steal
the bill so they can't pass it today. If
he steal it, they wouldn't be able to find
it to sign it. Some say, he was trying to
take it for the masses to see it and read
it. To see what really in it. But that
ent make no sense because everybody, who
could read, like Mzumbo and all his lawyer
friends, had copies of that bill already.
Still, some say, Colonel Brake and them
lie. They just wanted to lock up Greasy
at all cost. But they say, Pole ent name
Greasy for nothing. Wait and see! Also
we hear they take lawyer Edgar Maresse-
Smith, another people supporter. That was
a big joke. They lock him up because he
didn't park his carriage "straight" on the
road. They looking for any excuse. And Eva
and the Fat Lady tell just about everybody
to be in the Square opposite the Red House
today. It look like the whole town bite
the bait and it just about ready to start.

*(EVA is stopped, around a street corner,
by GREASY POLE, who grabs her by the waist
before she is able to move.)*

GREASY POLE

Is you I want to see.

EVA

(Startled) Yes?! *(Catching herself)* What
you doing out….here? Police everywhere.
You. . . see the man?

GREASY POLE

No fear. I give them the slip and slide.
Everything will be alright. I don't have
to hide. Come here.
(He pulls her tightly to his body).

EVA

Look! (*She holds him off*) Did you meet
the man, today?

GREASY POLE

I like it when you like this. Fiery!

EVA *(whispers)*

Watch out and keep your voice down. Today
is a big day. Everybody know that. *(He
tries to pull her to him again).* You
crazy? People up and about. I don't want
you to get caught again. You talk to the
man this morning? Is it on or off?

GREASY POLE

Easy, easy. Everything will be okay. You
can trust me.

EVA

I don't trust those bastards. *(Pause)* I
must know. I have to leave here now. You
forget….

GREASY POLE

It will be alright. (*Pause*) Okay?

EVA

Okay. (*She pulls away from him and leaves the area. He looks after her for a while.*)

ALCAZAR

(*Inside the Council Chamber. Up on the barricades.*)

You all know me, Henry A. Alcazar, a council member of long standing. The Right Honourable…. Whatever….Gentlemen, we are treading on very thin ice. Any minute now there will be uncontrollable crowds of people outside these chambers and they will insist that they be heard. Your charging a fee to get into the public gallery is not going to stop them. You will have to use policemen to control the crowd and try to thin it out somehow. I tell you, you will have to be constantly turning people away because they have no tickets. There will be an incredible build up of people at these chamber doors. You know what going to happen? Eh? We are talking about people of all walks of life. Respectable people, not just the so-called rabble. People will be all over the place. Even in the Square, all over. And you know why? Why? Because this bill is unjust. That is the crux of the matter and if that is so, then charging a fee to hear the debate will not make it just but will just ferment

further the discontent
that we know already exists out there.
Apart from all that, we also know that
this ticket business is illegal. What is
this? A dancehall or a theatre? Is this
a theatre show. A circus? Maybe we need
a Dancehall and Theatre Ordinance. No,
gentlemen, this is the Legislative Council
where the people's business is conducted.
You cannot charge them to be witness to
their own business. *(Loud roar outside.*
All this time the crowd has been building.)

TOURIST ANNIE

(Downstage. Observing RAM sleeping in the
other corner of the downstage area with
the placard which reads: **FIRE! FIRE! IN YUH**
WIRE*, draped over his head.)*
Look at RAM. And he well know the play
start, yes!

STEWART

I sure he have calcium stubs for teeth
by now. He always sleeping on that damp,
rotting concrete slab over there and just
grinding his teeth night and day.

(Roar of mob outside)

ALCAZAR (*In the Council Chamber*)

Gentlemen, gentlemen please, the police
may have to use their batons on the crowd.
Heaven forbid. Colonel Brake already has

constabulary members like flies out there.
I know some of them would love nothing
better. Some of them might even prefer
to use their pistols and bayonets on the
people. *(More noise from outside, from the
growing crowd)* . Please, please gentlemen,
let good sense prevail and let us adjourn
our business for today until this heat
cools off. *(Crowd noises)*. Gentlemen, I
withdraw from this debate, and with your
leave, I will now take my leave from these
chambers. *(More noise and shouts from the
rabble outside)*.

TOURIST ANNIE

*(Downstage looking at RAM who is still
sleeping)*
Every time they catch him they beat him up
and leave him for dead. *(Pause)* Is his
dreams. They grind down his dreams.

STEWART

What dreams?

TOURIST ANNIE

To be somebody one day. *(Pause)* *(Crowd
noises)*

STEWART

We all grind down one another's dreams.

TOURIST ANNIE

Just look around this town. All the others
dreaming about...

STEWART

...lost ambitions...to be rich and famous.

TOURIST ANNIE

No. Just to be somebody...to count. One
day.

STEWART

Yeah. (*Pause*) Hope is elusive...
(*Shouting voices emerge from the
barricades.*)

VOICES OFF

The Bill pass, the Bill pass, look Alcazar
leaving, the Bill done pass. (*Stones being
pelted etc...general ruction*).

HOLDER *(Voice off)*

Look these hooligans dragging the
Governor's carriage down to the sea! Stop
them! Stop them! Inspector! Inspector!
Inspector! Oh Lord, they throwing it in
the sea. My God man! What a disgrace!
What a shame! (*More stones on the
building.*)

FATHER/DARWENT approaches CHRISTINA/EVA.
Downstage at the fountain tub.

DARWENT

What you have for me…?

EVA

I don't know if this is a good idea, you
know. We shouldn't still be out here like
this. Something going to happen. I know…

DARWENT

I only wanted to….. *(Loud noise from the*
crowd)
So I came…. *(Pause)*

CHRISTINA

People say… No. People say it was
the drugs. Yes. Yes. No. But is the
pressure that split open my brain, yes.

FATHER

You don't have to…

CHRISTINA

It split my sense just so, down the middle.
Spread-eagle my heart apart. It was… It was
my lot to seek to spread love and suffer
for it. Sorry Daddy. I really sorry. You
use to walk so upright and respectable.

This is your little girl. But I good now,
you know. Since I meet Tourist Annie and
you, out here. *(Pause)*
(She dances as she sings)
The Moon
Too soon
Never came tonight
I was waiting
I was waiting
I was waiting
I was waiting
On my dream
To dance with the stars
Lights of my eyes
To dance in the skies
Light years to Mars
Oh…oh….

It had days back there when I didn't care.
Eventually I went with anything. Any
vibe. Any thing. And just like when I
dance, I fly! My spirit would soar with the
birds in the sky. So I coulda transport
myself anytime I wanted. With anybody. To
anywhere. The nuns at convent and in the
hospital prefer not to see it that way.
(Pause)
(She sings)

The moon
Too soon
Never came for spite
I was dancing
I was dancing
I was dancing

I was dancing
In my dream
To sing in the skies
To voice my prayers
To sing 'way my fears
With feet and eyes
(oh, oh…)

I know this ground, this pavement, like my own bed, my own head. Like your very spreadsheet I know this cold concrete, this rubble, is mine, my pillow. You have to know it, you know. You have to know it before it start to mean something to you. Once and for all you have to know this cold ground before it mean anything to you. I dance on this cold earth, you know. My bare feet warm up this cold earth. My soul warm up this cold earth. This is now my sacred earth, my sacred ground.
(Crowd noises. Pause)

Don't tell me we start to mean something already?

(They stare at each other. DARWENT moves slowly to embrace EVA and as they hug tightly they get more and more intense. This is very passionate, as the crowd seems to be getting very worked up. EVA and DARWENT are in the green Santa Cruz valley and can hear the crowd way in the distance in the city.)

EVA *(Quietly breaking away)*

You know they were planning to kidnap
Wrightson.

DARWENT

What?
(He jerks out of the embrace.
She laughs at his sudden reaction.)

EVA

Yes. That is what I hear. I don't know
how true… *(Pause.)*

DARWENT

Why you… entice me out here in this valley?

EVA

Why you come? Eh?

DARWENT   *(He embraces her again)*

To smell your cool, sea-green hills… of
Santa Cruz.

EVA

And? Yes.

DARWENT

To touch your seeds of bright grass, your
garden,
La Divina Pastora.

82

EVA

Yes. And?

DARWENT

To come down by your river. Oh Eva!
(They embrace and roll on the grass.)

EVA

For?….For?   *(Teasing him.)*

DARWENT

What you said was mine.

EVA

*(She snatches a piece of the clothes
she is supposed to be washing and
holds it in front of his face.)*
Which is? Which is?

DARWENT & EVA

Clothes!!!
*(They both laugh out loudly as their love
making gets really intense and grows to a
consummation.)*

EVA

Ah! Ah! *(Pause)* You smell something
burning?

DARWENT

(Surprised)
What?

EVA

Smoke?!
(She pulls herself together and can't hide her joy.)

DARWENT

The Red House! Oh no!
*(For a moment he is stunned as he pulls his pants up
and fixes himself)*

EVA

Oh! Oh! Oh! Oh! Neighbour oi!
Neighbour oi! *(Realising that GREASY POLE was successful.)*

DARWENT

You bitch! You knew they were going to do
this. You and your no-good friends. I am
the Goddam fire chief. The place is going
to burn flat if I am not there to give the
order.

EVA

Sure! You just like all the rest of them.
Why you come here? Eh? Eh?
*(She throws water from the tub/river and a
piece of wet clothes in his face.)*

To poke your little nasty washer-woman.
Eh?   Right?   Eh?

DARWENT

Shut up!   Good God!   I have to go.
*(He fumbles and gets on his burroquite
horse.)*

EVA

Well, let it burn.   Let it burn!   Let it
burn!
*(She shouts and laughs after him as he
gallops away, out of her green, lush
valley.   The skies turn red and dark with
flames and smoke.   She pulls on her red
dress and dances and shouts.   Shouts which
blend with the crowd as we get closer to
the burning building.)*

HOLDER *(Voice off)*

Smoke!   This smoke!   If I catch that witch...
*(He enters Stage Right from behind the
burning building and confronts EVA coming
from the Downstage area.   She sees him
before he sees her and she takes off Stage
Left behind the building.   She loses him.
He stumbles and coughs in the thick smoke.)*

TOURIST ANNIE *(Downstage on her stool.)*

Well the people saw Alcazar leave the house
and they thought, for sure, the bill was
passed.   And so they get more agitated
and that start the whole thing.   Now the

85

Sergeant have his hands full. He will look
for Eva, all over the place, for the rest
of today.
*(In the fire and on the barricades above,
GREASY POLE and EVA come through dancing
the limbo (dangerously) under some low
flaming rafters, not yet fallen. They sing:*
"Limbo, limbo, like me*….etc…."*
as they enjoy themselves.)

TOURIST ANNIE

*(She gets up and dances, matching their
dancing, downstage.)* Now that is what
the people want. Everywhere we go. That
is what they need. To defy gravity. To
find space for themselves where there is
none. *(She sings with GREASY POLE and EVA:*
"Limbo, Limbo, like me*…")*

(Enter FLETCHER hurriedly)

FLETCHER

Annie, this is ridiculous. Let me tell you
one time. They coming this morning to deal
with us. There is nothing I can do about
that now. Annie! Annie! You hear me?

TOURIST ANNIE

Listen, I started dancing and telling
stories in my mother's womb. Sonny boy, I
come from a respectable, Woodbrook family,
you know. *(Pause)* And they gave up on
me a long, long time ago too. You think
they studying me? They never study me. My

father, he never study me. He send me away
to study to be a doctor and not a dancer.
(She starts to whirl like a dervish) So
he tell my mother, "Cut her off! Mildred!
Cut her off! What she think it is at
all?" They leave me in the middle of Time
Square, with all the time in the world, but
nowhere… no place to go. Nothing… to do…
No! This is my home. So, I find my way back
and you know what he say? He say he don't
want to see me. He don't want to see me.
"You take my good, good, hard-earned money
and gone… and gone to America to dance?
To dance? To dance? Well look, you might
as well, you might as well go and skin up
and take man, Ah, ah, ah, ah! *(She holds
her belly and collapses as she groans in
pain.)* That is what he say. Yes, that
is what he say in front of me, in front of
my poor mother in the house. Ah, ah, ah,
ah! *(She cries lying flat on the ground.)*
(Pause) Well, I walk out of that house
that day in the hot sun and start to laugh…
. *(laughs and cries at the same time.)*   …
..start to laugh and I still laughing. I
still laughing because today you is my
family, boy. *(She holds on tightly to
FLETCHER.)* And here is my home. You know
what is family? They can't move us. They
can't move us. *(Pause)* Look, when I pick
up King Stewart from the roadside he didn't
know if he was going or coming. Look at
him now. Look at you! Look at you. And
the Syrian, neither his father nor his
brothers wanted to see him. They disown

him. And why? Eh? Why? We are family! *(She hugs him tightly again.)* Yes, I have family now. *(Pause)* Ram, where Ram going to go? And Christina's friends, walk pass her straight, right on this same street, here, everyday. They don't see her. When last they see her? My father. When last I see him? *(Pause)* Let God be the judge. *(Pause)* But this street here is where we belong, where I belong, where we must fight, where we always fight. Fletcher? You understand? *(She holds on to him and shakes him.)* You understand? *(She is almost delirious at this point.)* And this play Fletcher, boy, this play today, today, keeping us alive. Together. *(She turns calmly to her audience.)* Who will provide guidance and solace for these people? Eh? Tell me that? Who will teach them to be what they are? To believe in cottons and not silk. And still, look they could even make a little revenue, on the side, same time.

FLETCHER

Annie all that is fine.
At this very moment they coming.
They coming, today!

TOURIST ANNIE

I know how to stay one step ahead
of the authorities, darling.
(Taking in her audience of tourists.)
Some understand. Some don't.

FLETCHER

Annette Sylvester! Let's cut out this
shit! Once and for all! All right? They
exterminated that other group, on the All
Saints Cathedral site. All Saints!!!

TOURIST ANNIE

Fletcher! You are all bullshit and no
brains! You don't let them control you.
You adapt! Look, even those Anglicans
understand. Now, did they build back their
church after it burn flat a few years ago?
No!

FLETCHER

They now conduct all their business on
Direct TV.
But what that have to do with…?

TOURIST ANNIE

Right! Now. You have a part to play.
Okay?

FLETCHER

Where is Eva? You see Rachichacha?

TOURIST ANNIE

What. . . ?

FLETCHER

Don't worry.

Red House [Fire! Fire!]

(FLETCHER exits)

EVA & GREASY POLE

(They peep after him, then dance and sing.)
Fire, fire
And no water, water
Aye ya yai
Oh yo yoi *(repeat)*

(This dance is a fire pass dance as they appear to dance in the fire and transcend its heat. The fire appears to empower the people as they dance and sing. They seem possessed. It also seems to be a coquettish and enticing pique dance with a wiggling of hips and saucy earthiness between EVA and GREASY POLE. It becomes very erotic in the heat of the excitement. Suddenly, the music changes to a HINDU mantra as Ram (in his bandages) appears in the fire – cool, calm, collected. He is observed closely by the others as we hear voices hum the mantra. All of this only serves to aggravate the authorities even more.)

HOLDER

Where in hell is that damned Darwent?
Today, today, somebody going to pay.
Let me catch anyone of them. They have to pay.

(EVA and GREASY POLE have to scamper before SERGEANT HOLDER sees them. RAM

is left behind. HOLDER takes him away,
forcefully.)

JOE

*(Pulls CHRISTINA
to a downstage area.
They sit close, crouched together.)*
You seeing him?

CHRISTINA

Nah! He gone. What you find out? *(He
attempts to hold her close. It evolves
into a rough and tumble. She pushes him
off.)* What. . . you find out?

JOE

Look, after all these years, you know all
you still teasing people to eat that damn
apple. Well I tell them and I telling you
now I not eating that frigging big apple
again.

CHRISTINA

What you find . . . out?

JOE

What I find out? What I find out? That man
is a disgrace. That is what. He will do
for all of us. *(Pause)* If I don't do for
him first. *(Noises from the crowd.)*

CHRISTINA

Yes.

JOE

You know it was I who organise the sponsorship for the Heavy Metal Steelband, from Belmont nuh, when I was Managing Director at Industrial Steel. Now because of him the whole band in jail.

CHRISTINA

Don't worry that was a long time. . .

JOE

He was the one, with the other big Chinese gentleman, they make up all kind of lies about drugs and kickbacks and send information to headquarters in Germany and make me lose my position.

CHRISTINA

So you wasn't flying high with that big steel deal and scandal with those people from India and South Africa?

JOE

That happen while I was there but. . .

CHRISTINA

But what? *(Long pause) (JOE looks in her eyes and moves in slowly and nibbles*

*her ear.   They start to get intense, etc.
Crowd sounds of rising ruction at the
barricades.)*
*(FLETCHER, fully dressed as the Sergeant
Holder, bayonet in hand, enters and catches
them.)*

CHRISTINA

No.   This is not happening.

FLETCHER

After all these years you ent learn
nothing, boy.

CHRISTINA

Look Fletcher, you mean nothing to me.   You
understand?   Don't do anything stupid.

JOE

Is Fletcher you talking to you know.

FLETCHER

You have nothing to say.   You in no
position to tell me nothing.   (*Pause*)   You
have a wife, two healthy, good looking
teenage children . . .

CHRISTINA

Fletcher that was years ago . . .

FLETCHER

Shut up, woman!   *(Forcing the bayonet on
                    JOE)*
   You like woman?   Plenty woman?   Right?

CHRISTINA

Fletcher . . .

FLETCHER   *(Turns on CHRISTINA)*

What happen?   So you more hot than sweet
   and this can't satisfy you?   You want
more heat?   Eh?   Right here on this cold
ground?   Eh?   *(Stones and fire rage on the
                    barricades.)*

CHRISTINA

. . . the play. . .

FLETCHER

*(He spins around and cuts JOE on his
      shoulder with the bayonet.)*
         This is not play!!!

CHRISTINA

Oh Shit!   *(Pause)*

JOE   *(FLETCHER over him)*

Look there was a time when the high
life just full me up with coke.   *(Pause)*
Anything anybody wanted I use to get it
   for them.   Nothing was too much for me

to do for people. I use to like that.
(Pause) I learn that from my old Indian
grandmother, Naidu. As a boy in the
country I use to like her stories, of
nature, the forests, rivers and streams.
Rajputs and Aryans. Sacrifice and ancient
kingdoms. Knights, horsemen and wanderers.
Ancestors. How many of them remember? She
didn't care nothing. As a girl she run
off just so with Tacky, my grandfather,
a silent black man in the village who use
to say: "It have a story to tell, let your
imagine run wild." *(Pause)* Since I on
this street you know how many I see, like
fourteen year old Idi, get shoot down at
point blank range on Nelson Street, just
so. His guts splatter on the pavement
and all over me. He was a good child. I
see. . .   I see mummy die of despair and
despondence. I see myself pull everything
from under the feet of Althea and the
children. And you, Fletcher, you help
to drive me to all that. Yes. I was
responsible and stupid too. But now the
children and Althea safe in the States and
I here. That was hard to bear. I really
love that woman. . . and the kids, Stacey
and Lester jr. But at least I still here,
man, and could see and, and you know what?
. . . You know what? . . .   If only I
could really hate. . . I would hate you,
man. With all my heart. All my heart.
(He weeps) *(Pause)* But that is you.
. .*(CHRISTINA goes to him, pushes away
FLETCHER's bayonet and hugs him tightly.*

Red House [Fire! Fire!]

They appear very small in the corner.)

FLETCHER

All for a little play?   *(FLETCHER exits)*

STEWART/MZUMBO

(Raging fire on the barricades, dressed as Mzumbo.) Citizens, this is a cleansing fire. If this society won't let us live morally with them, then we will have to live with them immorally.

TOURIST ANNIE   *(From downstage)*

King Stewart? Where you get that speech? That is not in my text. What you talking about? You should be in hiding. If the authorities find you, they will kill you and you must understand that as a leader you are needed alive.

MZUMBO/STEWART

This is a time of crisis. It is now too late for all that old talk. Fire is burning man, pull your own weight. Now sing with me. My people!
(He chants while doing the 'Pay De Devil' dance.)
I must not be afraid
To re-invent the wheel
(Chorus) I will fear no evil

I must not be afraid
To re-invent the wheel

(Chorus) I will fear no evil.

In the heat of the battle you have to know
who you are and what you have to do. No
time for you, the wicked, to weep for your
gold. Jah! Mercedes is melting. Oh yes!
What a Big Molten Wickedness, melting,
melting. We are purifying this sacred
space for the people. Jah Rastafari! Ever
living. Ever faithful. . . *(He chants)*
I must not be afraid
I know I am the seed
I must not be afraid
For that is what we need
(Chorus) For I will fear no evil

I must not be afraid
I know I am the seed
I must not be afraid
For that is what we need
(Chorus) I will fear no evil . . . Burn
them!

TOURIST ANNIE

Stewart, get to hell out of here! Come
on, man. *(To her audience)* Don't mind the
King. Mzumbo Lazare was a man of law and
order, all this time he really in hiding.
*(Motions to STEWART for him to leave the
stage.)*
The authorities read the Riot Act and
frantically trying to find Captain *(Fire
Brigade)* Darwent to put out the fire.
Meanwhile the members of the constabulary
start to fire at people, wild and

unnecessarily, up and down the place and
kill 16 people and wound about 43. Many
of whom are washer-women. There is an
absolutely unjustified use of the bayonet.
And people scampering madly from the Public
Square to the sanctuary of the Cathedral.
The Bishop standing at the door and taking
them in. In the meantime, Colonel Brake
and his men getting the Governor and
Walsh Wrightson, Director of Public Works,
safely out of the Red House. They dress
Mr. Wrightson, as a woman and right now
Sergeant Tom Holder is trying to sneak him
out of the house. Eva in her red dress,
as you have seen, is all around, on the
scene and doing her best to keep out of
the Sergeant's way. *(An old woman is seen
in the smoke in the midst of the building.
We see EVA nearby, as if approaching
the woman. A loud shot goes off. EVA
screams and drops to the ground. TOURIST
ANNIE holds her belly. The old woman
disappears.)*

(ALL FREEZE)

*(TOURIST ANNIE leaves her space and races
into the smoke. Commotion everywhere. She
emerges out of the smoke with EVA in her
arms. EVA is dead. TOURIST ANNIE stands
in the middle of the barricades. A MOKO-
JUMBIE, The God of Retribution, appears.
TOURIST ANNIE moves downstage carrying EVA
in her arms.) (Pause)*
(She breaks down and lets out a piercing

scream.)

No! No! No!!! Sergeant Holder, in a blind
jealous rage, suppose to stab Eva with the
bayonet after he gets Wrightson out of the
Red House. What is this? Oh God! No!
No! Who shooting gun in this place?
Ram! Ram! Fletcher!!!
*(Pause) (She slowly begins to sing
The Song In Praise of CHRISTINA's Spirit.)*

If you was a real man
You woulda die so, die so
If I was a woman
Ah shoulda die so, so oh

If you did know sorrow
You shoulda say so, say so
If you did feel sorrow
Why you didn't say so, so oh

When she rings the bell
We will all know, all know
When he rings the bell
We go all go, go oh

We will multiply
We must testify

No one can say why
Everyone can see why

There's no other way
What else can we say (*repeat*)

(*They all gather except FLETCHER and RAM.*)
(*After a while FLETCHER enters.*)

FLETCHER

Where Rachichacha?
(*Shortly after, RAM enters. FLETCHER jumps him.*)
Traitor!!!
(*JOE attacks FLETCHER, the others try to separate them as TOURIST ANNIE just looks on and keeps singing.*)
You did this to us!
(*RAM is on the ground, helpless. They all look to TOURIST ANNIE, who holds CHRISTINA, dead in her lap, as she sings her plea to the audience. JOE, finally realising what has happened, lets go of FLETCHER, rushes over and holds on to CHRISTINA tightly. FATHER is busy chanting prayers to himself, making a rhythm, fingering the beads and a cross in his hands. The Song In Praise of CHRISTINA's Spirit continues plaintively to the audience of tourists.*)

VOICES

We must testify
We must multiply

No one can say why
Everyone can see why

There's no other way
What else can we say (*repeat*)

(TOURIST ANNIE rings the bell.)

FADE

End of ACT II

ACT III: The TRIAL

Most of the fire has subsided. RAM, still bandaged, is alone searching through the rubble. FLETCHER enters and startles him. RAM snatches a piece of stick to pursue FLETCHER. He runs after him. FLETCHER picks up a stick of his own and wards off RAM, who uses a dustbin-cover as a shield. (RAM dances gatkha as FLETCHER dances calinda) They exchange blows for a while.

CHORUS

Ah don't know what you do
But they send me for you
(*repeat*)

(TOURIST ANNIE enters and upon seeing them attempts to stop them by charging expertly into this stickfight meeting.)

TOURIST ANNIE

Cut this out! All of you! Cut it out!

FLETCHER

Annie! Annie! Is you cause this you know. I warn all you to leave this space, leave the people place. . .

TOURIST ANNIE

Who people place? This is our space.

FLETCHER

Your place? That is the same nonsense
that you and that monkey man, King Stewart,
always talking. And you know that his wife
butt all the sense out of his head a long
time ago, till he spitting backwards and
all.

TOURIST ANNIE

This here is the People's Parliament, the
People's Court.

FLETCHER

All you does believe everything them people
tell all you. What Parliament? What
people?

TOURIST ANNIE

Tell we? Tell me? Nobody ent tell me
nothing.

FLETCHER

So where that idea come from then?

TOURIST ANNIE

What idea?

FLETCHER

All this horse shit about People's
Parliament and People's Court. Look,

the only reason they allow you to run a People's Court down here is because it was a way to ease up the regular courts. And if we could run we own thing down here and they don't have to deal with us and our little shitty squabbles at all, then it is better for them.

(RAM rushes FLETCHER with his stick and is able to get in a good blow before TOURIST ANNIE wards him off.)

TOURIST ANNIE

They don't care if we all die off or kill each other off anyway.

(Enter KING STEWART, JOE and FATHER cautiously.)

FLETCHER

I hold you and Tomboy *(Points to STEWART)* here responsible for what happened to Christina.

STEWART

Who put you up to this?

FLETCHER

Don't look at me. Ask Rachichacha. If you *(points to TOURIST ANNIE)* had any guts or decency, you would put your own self on trial in your People's Court. For the murder-

FATHER

What?   *(Long pause)*

STEWART

Don't do it, Annie.

JOE

It is part of the plot they set up with Fletcher.

STEWART

They want us to look like fools in front of all these people. They want us to discredit ourselves in front of all the world.

FATHER

Yes, Annie! This is a mockery, a mimicry, set up by the Council Men. Can't you see? They have an international crisis on their hands, and if they can make us look stupid in front of these very tourists so they won't come back, that would be an easy way to have us terminated, annihilated, destroyed. I know these people.

FLETCHER

You all speak out of the both sides of your face at the same time. You talk all the time about justice. You were the ones to convict Bitter Man Singh and Rugged Lloyd, big people killers out here. But

now I see, you just like all the others.
You want it your way and that is it.
Rachichacha here is your man.

JOE

And your man is in St. Joseph?

FLETCHER

Why you went to St. Joseph?

JOE

Was it an M-16 or the German Super Luger?
Eh?
Bagshot, the funeral agency man, right?
"You shoot them, we bag them".

TOURIST ANNIE

Stop it! *(Pause)* I will do it.

STEWART

No Annie. Don't. . .

FLETCHER

Coward!
All yuh so,
you and them council men,
always hiding behind the law.
The rule of law!
All yuh run around and manufacture
democratic rule over we,
then yuh manufacture democratic law to hold
we.

"Yuh make a mockery of the law
and have the law protect yuh same time."

TOURIST ANNIE

Well if that is the plot then I have to do
it . . .

FATHER

Do you know what you are doing?

TOURIST ANNIE

But I have one condition.

FLETCHER

Which is?

TOURIST ANNIE

Ram, the Silent God, must sit as the Judge.
Assisted by you Father.

FLETCHER

For God's sake, he is just a 2.00 am street
sweeper! We do not need an idler to tell
us that we are small down here and the sky
is large up there. (*Pause*) I see. He
will-

STEWART

Annie, let us talk about this.

TOURIST ANNIE

There is nothing to talk about, King. He
is right. We cannot have one law for some
and then another for others.

JOE

But he is a set-up man. This is not
justice.
We should try him for . . .

TOURIST ANNIE

Yes, this is a set-up. And he is right.
It all points to me. I must clear my name
in front of all these people.

STEWART

Clear what name? Who is asking you to
clear your name? And from what? This is
ridiculous. Everybody knows Tom Holder
viciously killed Eva out of jealousy and we
are discussing putting Annie on trial? You
should put me on trial instead. I am the
leader here. What? You are giving up your
Queen? Sheer madness!

FLETCHER

And you and Mr. Magic Machine here know
about that.
Tell it to the court, Sirs.

JOE

This is really a domestic issue.

TOURIST ANNIE

*(She takes out a banner, which reads THE
PEOPLE'S COURT.)* Come on fellas! Help me
with this. *(They put it up and start to
arrange the space for the court proceedings
to take place.)* King Stewart, you will be
my lawyer and argue my case.

JOE

I can take the stand on your behalf.

TOURIST ANNIE

I am sure, Fletcher, you have your case
against me prepared.

FLETCHER

Not just you.

STEWART

Isn't this going too far?

FLETCHER

Not far enough! Not far enough. Right
Silent God?
(RAM is aggravated.)

TOURIST ANNIE

Don't forget, Father, you have to assist
Ram in this.
*(RAM is set up in the centre of a semi-
circle of people with the banner on the*

*barricades behind their heads. He knocks
his gavel to bring the court to order.
Throughout RAM makes what sounds he can and
they are interpreted by FATHER.)*

RAM

Ahhhhhhhha! AAAAAAA ord arch! ! !

FATHER

Wait! Before we start. Anybody have
anything to eat?

FLETCHER

What happen, you didn't get enough from
your washerwoman? *(Pause)*

FATHER

Okay! Okay!
We are called to order today on this day of
our Lord the 23rd of March. *(consults with
RAM)*

FLETCHER

Oho, I thought you were going to say a
prayer.

RAM

(Gesticulating madly, pointing to himself.)
Orrrrrrr! Orrrrrr! Ammmm! Eeeyah ayyy.
Yeah.

FATHER

Order! The People's Court of Manohar
Dookie, Ram, The Silent God, is now in
session. Today we have a very serious case
to hear. Mr. Prosecutor, kindly read the
case please.

FLETCHER

Thank you. As it pleases the People's
Court with due respect and decorum. The
case today is: The People Against Tourist
Annette Sylvester for atrocities committed
on this day against the people themselves.

STEWART

Atrocities? Annie, we can't go on with
this.

FATHER

King Stewart, as the person representing
Defendant Annette Sylvester, do you wish to
address the court at this time?

STEWART

Yes! Sir. . .

FLETCHER

Objection! ! !

FATHER

Not yet, man!

FLETCHER

I have to establish my case first.

STEWART

But we done know what you coming with . . .

(RAM moves from behind his desk and pelts his gavel at FLETCHER's head. He just misses. FATHER has to contain RAM and put him back in his chair.)

TOURIST ANNIE

(Taking charge)
I will have no more of this in my court. Regardless of what you all might think, this is a respectable People's Court. No more of that! You hear me? All of you! And that goes for you too, Chief Flying Hammer. Is obvious you not accustomed being in a position or office of power, for that matter. So watch it!

RAM

Arkh oou ooh?

FATHER

Mr.   Persecutor . . .Prosecutor. .   .

FLETCHER

Thank you, kind sirs. Mam. I have information that there was a plot afoot, there was a well-organised plan to put fire

to Government House. Rush the main town.
And seize the chief fort and arsenal. This
was indeed a slave rebellion organised by
Tomboy and Tacky here. *(Points to JOE)* I
also know for a fact that Tourism Nanny
instigated and imposed on these people
a collective oath which holds all the
conspirators to secrecy and loyalty and
that they are therefore all responsible for
this uprising.
(Uproar)
An uprising, ladies and gentlemen, which
resulted in the death of Eva Carvalho and
others, ladies and gentlemen. In their
oath, my lord, they vow to put on the port
and mien suitable to affecting the dignity
of Kings. Now, ask me this thing. This
was just a crazed fantasy based on a mere
lust for power and hopes of lawless liberty
and rights.

JOE

Annie! I can't take this.

TOURIST ANNIE

Magic machine! Keep quiet. Sit. . . down!

FATHER

Is that your case? Sir.

FLETCHER

That ent enough?
Is long time now they planning this thing.

RAM

Ahhhhh!

FATHER

Council for the defendant.

STEWART

My lord, what we have here is the Council
Men seeking to pay back a debt for the
privilege of warming those benches in the
house. What we have is men in jobs. Men
who have to look for jobs and to keep those
jobs when they find them. I had a job once.
It is one generation's short-term lease on
life. That is what a job is. But surely,
my lord, this is about more than job.
(Pause) Sergeant Tom Holder had a job to
do. People like him never trust people.
Never believe in people. Never commit to
people. Tom Holder never was capable of
making a commitment to anyone or anything,
except to a contempt for himself. *(To
FLETCHER)* You use your very style to show
your contempt for your own self. And it
was by killing Christina that he was trying
to . . .

FLETCHER

EVA! . . . Your honour, I object!
Irrelevant and misleading. . . what does
that have to do with Nanny?

115

FATHER

Yes! Sustained. You are making this very
confusing. Please stick to the matter in
the palm of your hand.
I know my catechism.

STEWART

Your Honour, it is the clinging and blood-
sucking grapevine of sexual power games
that does strangulate a good woman like Eva
Carvalho. Tom Holder could never conceive
of a space for justice existing outside
of certain imperial organs. *(Pause)* Now
we have meters for water. Why introduce
this tax? Everyone has to pay because some
want more. More and more. *(Pause)* I call
Tourist Annie to the stand. *(She takes the
stand.)*

FATHER

State your name, please.

TOURIST ANNIE

Annette Sylvester.

FATHER

By the power invested in me by this
People's Court, do you swear on this sacred
ground, sanctified by the eternal flame, to
tell the whole truth and nothing but the
truth?

TOURIST ANNIE

I do.

FATHER

You will now kiss the ground.
(She kneels and kisses the ground.)

STEWART

What is your story?

TOURIST ANNIE

The Hummingbird is at its moment of ecstasy when it enters the flower. When it pollinates the flower. *(Pause)* You can only add to the circle of life as you see it. A commodius vicus of recirculation.
(Pause)
Circular, bircular. *(Pause)*

FATHER

Yes. Do you wish to ask any questions?
(To FLETCHER)

FLETCHER

Why do you insist on being a reject of destiny?

TOURIST ANNIE

You don't understand, do you? There is no race.

FLETCHER

What is it then?

TOURIST ANNIE

I love the position I have been given. . .

FLETCHER

Which is?

TOURIST ANNIE

. . . as lowly outsider.

STEWART

A lonely runaway with the maroons. . .

FLETCHER

Tomboy!

STEWART

. . . from the chains of Babylon. And
nestled in my mother's yard in Belmont, in
Dahomey. (*He sings*)
All the way from Africa land
Coming to hear them pray *(say)*
Coming, coming
Coming, coming
Coming to hear them pray *(say)*

*(They all join in the singing and go into a
trance*

except *FLETCHER)*

(PAUSE.)

FATHER

Miss Annette Sylvester you may step down
now.

STEWART

I call Lester Joseph McLean (alias Magic
Machine) to the witness stand.

JOE

I kiss this sacred ground and swear to talk
the truth and nothing but the truth.

RAM

Eeee orry! Your oory!

JOE

Okay, wait. The Council Men paid Fletcher
good money, he and Captain Baker, to help
them remove the street people without
making the usual mess. Not just from our
site but the street people all over the
city. Fletcher had planned to scare us
away somehow. Maybe by killing one or
two of us. This strategy of his is well
known. He, as we well know, has always had
access to guns of all types. What as an
ex-policeman and all. . . At one point
it seemed as though I would be his target.
But they don't call me Magic Machine for

119

nothing. You see when you dealing with
me, they don't know who they dealing with.
(TOURIST ANNIE clears her throat) They may
have planned to kill even Ram. We know now
it was Christina. *(Overcome by sadness)*
Poor Christina!

STEWART

We know that Tom Holder had it in for Eva.

JOE

The idea was that nobody cares about us
anyway, so, if one or two are killed,
the society people wouldn't even know
or care. *(Pause)* So the plan was for
Fletcher to drunken and gag Ram. He was
sleeping all day, remember? Get him out
of the way. Then Fletcher, himself, was
to put on Ram's Walsh Wrightson old woman
costume and go into the smoke and shoot
Eva. Bodoi! We would not see Sergeant
Holder around because he would be dressed
as the woman. And because we knew Ram
was supposed to play the old woman, the
only person we could blame for the murder
would be Ram himself. We already know
that Fletcher here was jealous of Eva and
Greasy Pole. The sudden bloody turn of
events would upset all of us, we would turn
on poor Ram and move on. Leave this space
forever. Fletcher would collect his blood
money and the Council Men would be spared
the mess of extermination and an incident
of international proportions. And that is

exactly what took place.

FATHER

Mr. Tom Holder.

FLETCHER

So you, a known, slippery, dougla snake
about the place, know that is what happen?

JOE

Yes.

FLETCHER

Alright! So all of all you, led by Nanny
and Sambo, didn't take some kind of old,
some devil oath to go and burn down the
people house?

JOE

Absolutely n. . .

STEWART

Objection! Leading on the witness. . .

FLETCHER

Alright. Alright.

FATHER

Step down, Mr. Magic.

FLETCHER

Now, if you were to say that the Council
Men asked me to help them in this
situation, you would be right. I am the
only one here they can talk to. Yes! If
you were to say that there were plans in
place to kill us and in that way remove
us all from this site, you would be right.
But, no! If you were to say that I wanted
to kill somebody, you would, definitely,
be wrong. I have never, at anytime, been
involved in that kind of activity. *(They
laugh out loudly)* Ask anybody who has
known me over the years. Ladies and
gentlemen, I remind you that I begged Annie
to lead us all out of this. She never paid
heed. None of you all ever listened. I
pleaded with each one of you, separately
and collectively. No one listened. After
a while the Council Men got fed up. Fed
up, ladies and gentlemen. Yes, fed up.
They had asked me to help and it seemed
to them that I, that I, was doing nothing.
Nothing, ladies and gentlemen. Making
no headway. Colonial Logic was a chip
on the Council Men shoulders. And with
that pressure weighing them down they
called in Colonel Brake, Captain Baker
and the National Guard. Now once they
come in you know what that means? Action!
Action. Ladies and gentlemen. Action.
They came down this morning and kidnapped
me and threw me in a cell and never even
told me of their plans. So they took me
out of commission. Yes. Out . . . of.

122

. . commission, ladies and gentlemen. I could warn nobody anymore. They then entered into the play and shot Christina. *(Consternation in the court.)* That is why, that is why, I was not here at the time. But Ram was here. They may even have paid Ram to do the job. *(A rough and tumble, RAM knocks his gavel.)* I don't know how. . . how they did it. Because all of you know that Silent God use to be a double agent. A man with a forked tongue. Now Christina is dead. *(FLETCHER rushes up to TOURIST ANNIE. He is held back.)* She is responsible, ladies and gentlemen. Who else can be responsible? *(Pause.)* I rest my case. *(Rowdy argument in the court ensues.)*

FATHER

Order! Come on, order! Order! *(RAM screams out and everyone comes to order.)* I think the positions have been made very clear. Ladies and gentlemen, Justice Ram will now retire to ponder his verdict.

(RAM and FATHER huddle in a corner.)

TOURIST ANNIE

You see that? This place will always defy Colonial Logic. They going to have a hard time.

FLETCHER

You try to defy the bottom line.

TOURIST ANNIE

People like you always talk about the
bottom line like if is God 'self you
talking about.

STEWART

All of our bottoms are on the line. And
have been for a long time and even Colonial
Logic cannot save us now. *(Pause)*

FLETCHER

So who will pay for all this?

TOURIST ANNIE

I thought you wanted me to. That is
why I agreed to it. *(Pause)* (*She sits
in a stooping position, holds on to her
belly.*) A woman must make sacrifices for her
family. I must bleed time and time again
for my offspring. *(She beats her chest
repeatedly.)* *(Pause.)* I will pay. Don't
worry, I will pay. That is what I have to
do. If somebody have to pay, somebody have
to pay. We serious now. *(Pause.)*

FLETCHER

Why did you pursue this? Why did we pursue
this? Why couldn't you and your people
just move on? I never wanted it to come
to this. You know people always get in the
way.

STEWART

You should have thought of that when we were young. We had a chance to choose in those days. Today our children are paying for our selfishness and our lack of vision. Now it is too late. Now they wouldn't even let us. . .

FATHER

Order! Order! Order please! Justice Ram has reached a verdict. Order! Order please! Order! Ladies and gentlemen, order! Will the defendant Annette Sylvester (a.k.a. Tourist Annie) charged with the pre-meditated murdered of Eva Carvalho please step forward. The People's Court of Manohar Dookie, Ram, The Silent God, finds the defendant guilty and is sentenced to be exterminated at sun. . .

FLETCHER

(He flies at RAM's throat.)
I tell you I did never trust this focking Indian!!!
(RAM laughs hysterically at FLETCHER as STEWART blocks FLETCHER'S attack.)

STEWART

Wait! Hath not a Jew eyes!?

FLETCHER *(to RAM)*

Who cut out your tongue, eh?

I suppose you blame African people for
that!

STEWART

His own people do that to him.

FLETCHER *(to STEWART)*

I suppose you blame your own people for
that too!

FATHER

So what?

STEWART

When negro people was in power on this
island,
African people get nothing.

FATHER

So what?

JOE

And then when the Indians take power,
African people still get nothing.

FLETCHER *(to JOE)*

And you blame Indian people for that.

FATHER

So focking what?

Nothing is more real than nothing!
We begin again from what we know, nothing.
(Pause.)
Anybody have anything to eat?

TOURIST ANNIE

Yuh know, the people should decide.
The people should be the jury.

FLETCHER *(Agitated)*

What people now?

TOURIST ANNIE

The people. *(Points to her audience of
tourists.)*

STEWART

You mean these people here?

FLETCHER *(In disbelief.)*

But they don't know what really happening
with us.
They don't even really live out here.

STEWART

Yes! Why should they decide, Annie?

*(RAM pulls a blade out of his clothes and
attacks FLETCHER. The others have to subdue
RAM.)*

TOURIST ANNIE

(Goes over to RAM to pacify him.)
Okay Ram, okay. Easy. *(Smiling at
FLETCHER.)*
Sydney Fletcher, I am willing to go on the
first sun up.
I will meet Christina and we will talk.
In fact I talk to her a lot already.

FLETCHER

You talk to Christina?

TOURIST ANNIE

Yes. All the time.
Oh yes, I communicate with Eva all the
time.

CHRISTINA   *(Off-stage voice)*

Sergeant! Holder, darling.

TOURIST ANNIE
Eva!

FLETCHER

What the. . . *(He is confused. He tries to
run. The 12 foot tall fiery apparition of
EVA in her red dress, the figure of death,
appears as dark ominous clouds gather
overhead.)*

TOURIST ANNIE

Eva, leave him alone.

128

CHRISTINA

Where did the gun come from, Holder? The
M-16. Wasn't it supposed to be a bayonet?
According to history, remember? A bayonet
 between the ribs. The one rib you give
me. Eh, Sergeant? *(The apparition pursues
him.)*

FLETCHER

No! No! No!

TOURIST ANNIE

It's okay. Eva. *(The apparition does not
let up.)* Eva! Eva!! Eva!!!! That's enough!
I said, that's enough!!
*(The apparition reluctantly disappears. The
clouds lift. Things appear normal again.)*

FLETCHER

What was that? You hear her? Right?

STEWART

What was what?

FLETCHER

You ent see nothing?

JOE

No. You see something? *(Pause)*

FLETCHER

Yeah. Like a dragon fighting a dove in the sky. Father? *(Silence)* *(He remains motionless on the ground.)*
What is this? Some kind of spirit business?

STEWART *(Whispers.)*

Obeah. *(Pause)*

FLETCHER

That woman. That woman. Eva! Eva! Eva! *(Pause)* You know what I am? A policeman. A shitting policeman doing these people work. Their dirty work. Then this woman come and is like she wash my life clean. She make my soul feel fresh. She give me new life, just to think of her, just to touch her. And then, and then, she gone with him. Greasy Pole. Of all people, she gone with Greasy. I spend good money on that woman and imagine she gone with Pole. Greasy? Is like she just hang me out to dry. *(Weeps.)* What sense any of this make? Nothing ent making no sense in this place. Is only dirty work. Dirty work. But I didn't do it. Is the council men. It must be sly Ram and them evil dragon men that do it, I tell you.

TOURIST ANNIE

Go and collect your money. *(She sings quietly.)*

130

Ah don't know what you do
But they send me for you.   *(Repeat)*

FLETCHER   *(Holds his head and screams.)*

Ah didn't do nothing. Oh God, all you. Ah
didn't do nothing. Nothing! Ah didn't do
nothing! Nothing!
(The song continues.)

FADE

END OF ACT III

EPILOGUE: THE FUNERAL

EVA's body is brought out wrapped in white cotton and placed flat on RAM's cart. The body is adorned with red roses.

TOURIST ANNIE *(To the audience)*

We have to remember to tell the stories that we are told, that happened, that we live through and we create. And we see other people doing. And how we come to think about things the way we do. For that is how we continue to hold on to our space in the world.

By the way, Emmanuel Lazare *(For that was Mzumbo's name)* and the others were charged for burning down the Red House but were acquitted by December of the same year. A victory for the people. *(Pause.)*

The next show is in two hours, right here in this Public Square. The Little Theatre must push on through. *(Pause.)* Tom Holder was also tried and acquitted for the murder of Eva. We will bury our dead.

(A funeral procession for EVA CARVALHO moves off with a spirited soulful dirge created by the mourners, JOE, FATHER, FLETCHER and TOURIST ANNIE. CHRISTINA brings up the rear.)

(RAM is left in the centre of the rubble and dirt contemplating his navel and

Red House [Fire! Fire!]

humming.   KING STEWART stands over him for
a while and then gets down and joins his
humming.)

FADE

END OF EPILOGUE

Sunshine Suite Tobago
July 28th, 1997

Hartford, Connecticut
May 17th, 1998

Port of Spain, Trinidad
June 22nd, 1999

MUD !

a ritual in mud and percussion

"I participate, therefore I am."
-Leslie Desmangles-

". . . emphasis is on the human . . . .
Divine enlargement of the human condition
should be viewed dramatically, through man.
The mode for this is Ritual. The medium is
Man. Ritual equates the divine (superhuman)
dimension with the communal will, fusing,
the social with the spiritual . ...the
ritual, sublimated or expressive, is both
social therapy and reaffirmation of group
solidarity, a hankering back to the origins
and formation of guilds and phratries.
Man re-affirms his indebtedness to earth,
dedicates himself anew to the demands
of continuity and evokes the energies
of productivity. Re-absorbed within the
communal psyche he provokes the resources
of Nature; he is in turn replenished for
the cyclic drain in his fragile individual
potency."

-Wole Soyinka-

MUD!

In Memory of Lise Waxer

A NOTE

The following simple ideas should definitely be ignored if you have your own understanding of Jouvay Process, which manifests itself when the principles of creativity embedded in the survival strategies of the emancipation tradition are invoked. Then you will be able to come up with your own simple ideas based on this understanding. Therefore, what is recorded here, for those interested in the process, is what one group did for a MUD! ritual. It is a rough guide. It cannot be a prescription. It is meant to help others create and participate in, from time to time, with their communities, their own MUD! rituals.

- Four Simple Ideas -

1.   Devotees to the MUD! ritual are asked
to give themselves initiation names, which
they feel reflect their deep inner selves.
If any devotees are unable to do this,
then the other devotees can all agree on
names, for them, in a naming ceremony.
The naming ceremony is only done for those
devotees unable to do it for themselves.
The devotees will enter the ritual in the
presence of their community with their new
initiation names. New initiation names are
required every time the ritual is practiced
because the MUD! ritual is a communal
ritual of self-renewal, to re-enter and
come out of the womb of the earth afresh, a
ritual of the sunrise, the dawn, a virtual
jouvay.

2.   Devotees are asked to use the event
of the MUD! ritual to re-trace those
experiences of their lives which they deem
to be critical turning points or junctures
which account for the persons they see
themselves to be at the time of the MUD!
ritual. Duration: Within one hour at a
time, unless otherwise determined.

3.   Devotees are asked to re-trace these
experiences through percussion (with
instruments and/or the body), mud, mime,
song, dance, movement, music, poetry,
poetic rhythm, costume, gesture, dialogue,
monologue or role-play in keeping with

the mythologies of the popular cultures of the devotees and their communities. These experiences might be from the distant past, from dreams, from the immediate past or even from present pre-occupations imagined or a dreamed-of future. Very little or nothing is to be written down. Definitely no script is written up or committed to memory.

4.   Devotees are asked to use local mud, always local. The mud is to be procured and cleaned, if at all possible, by the devotees themselves and put into wooden or clay bowls in the form of balls, one for each devotee.

MUD!

MUD! was created and first performed
at Trinity College, Hartford, CT
on Monday October 22nd 2001 by:

Saijayananda Madivala (Hercules S)
Ramsay Saunders (Strawberry)
Peter Votto (Purple Haze)
Amanda Waxman (Buttercup)

Led by Tony Hall (Lordstreet)
Music by Lise Waxer
& The Latin Ensemble (Salsaficacion)

THE ENTRÉE

THE CAST

(Sings)
There's a meeting here tonight
There's a meeting here tonight
Come one come all and join around
There is a meeting here tonight . . .

1. THE BIRTH - Prologue

A large transparent membrane.

VOICE

In the beginning there was the petri
dish
And it was clean.
On the surface lay
The impermeable, impenetrable,
impregnable
Transparent culture.
Nothing was stirring, not even the
tinniest
Of the tinniest.

*A shadow, in the image of a huge gloved hand,
projects itself slowly over the membrane.*

All was still until the hand of the
creator cast a dark shadow over the
petri dish.
The hand stood erect, each long firm

MUD!

```
    digit wrapped safely in the protective
    latex
    Of a disinfected, bulletproof
    Politically correct, anti-terroristic
    Ribbed for pleasure, sanitized glove.

    Within seconds
    The hand reached out and obeying the
    urge
    To close itself, it squeezed a drop
    Of primordial ooze, a pustule
    Of sweet nectar, into the peaceful
    Slumbering culture, provoking
    A chain reaction.
```

Pulsing begins and increases to a dizzying intensity until the membrane bursts and the oozy creatures of skin and bones emerge slimy and slippery from the membrane. The devotees, as babies, are born screaming themselves into the dawn of life.

2. DREAM TRANSITION

Devotees grow slowly to be little children and find themselves in a museum of human artifacts looking for their fathers and mothers.

VOICES

Daddy! Daddy! Mummy! Mummy!
(*Then older*) Dad!? Dad?! Mom?! Mom?!

3. EARLY CHILDHOOD

*Devotees stand in their corners and recite
Walt Whitman. They take their mud balls
out of the receptacles and roll them gently
in their hands as they deliver the poetry
of childhood and growing up. They roll
the mud balls onto the plastic membrane,
the globe of the world. This is baby play.
As they roll these mud balls they each
recite excerpts from Walt Whitman's "There
Was a Child Went Forth" (Whitman, Walt.
"Leaves of Grass", New York: Viking Penguin
Inc.1959.)*

> "The early lilacs became part of this
> child,
> And grass, and white and red
> morningglories, and white and red
> clover, and the song of the phoebe-
> bird,
> And the March-born lambs, and the sow's
> pink-faint litter, and the
> mare's foul, and the cow's calf, and
> the noisy brood of the
> barnyard or by the mire of the pondside
> . . and the fish
> suspending themselves so curiously
> below there . . . and the
> beautiful curious liquid . . and the
> water-plants with their
> graceful flat heads . . all became part
> of him."

Balloons of different colours, filled with

MUD!

water, are suspended as mobiles over this play. The devotees stretch up to reach, to touch, to play with the balloons. They are unable to reach them.

Eventually after much effort they are able to break the balloons and the water from the balloons shower down on them. The devotees play in the ooze that is created between the mud balls and the water.

It is playtime.

Children playing in mud. Parents struggle to keep them clean. The devotees discover the slippery, slimy mud and what they can do to each other with it. They become animals in the mud. Some prefer not to get dirty-innocent children. Others wallow in it-dirty children. Mud cakes are created. They eat mud cakes. Face down, they fight in the mud. They paint each other lavishly with the mud. The group evolves its own early childhood mud scenario.

4. LATE CHILDHOOD

One of the mud cakes turns into a huge cigarette.

STRAWBERRY

I smoked my first cigarette when I was 14. I was with my best friend of the time, Natalie. She stole two from her dad- the town drug addict, the black sheep of the country club circuit. We sat at the end of the dock on lake Minnetonka, the sun setting, our feet dangling into the water. I was so nervous I dropped my cigarette in the water and we were forced to share, which was probably a good thing considering her father smoked Marlboro Reds. We were so scared of being caught that we ran home and jumped in my back yard pool with all of our clothes and our shoes on so my mom wouldn't suspect anything. (*Pause.*) Less than a year later Natalie's father killed himself. His son found him in the garage with the engine running. . . . . Natalie was never the same after that. She lost her ambition, stayed at home, following her drug addict boyfriend around. Her worst nightmares came true. As for me, I smoked for three years after that.

5. ADOLESCENCE

Females enact, in slow mime, first awareness of sexual selves and flirting. Any conceived appropriate text can be inserted here. Males do a heavy macho dance around the young nubile females and simulate an act of snatching them away and taking them to the ground initiating the sex act.

MUD!

Freeze.

Males tell dreams experienced as they discovered the growing of their penises and what they could do with them. Jockey shorts action.

Females tell dreams experienced as they discovered their breasts refusing to grow and what that meant to them.
Bra action.

BUTTERCUP

Look at me . . . sixteen years old .
. . and I look as underdeveloped as a twelve year old. I mean where are my curves. My mom has curves . . . she must be one of the curviest women I know . . . and my grandmother . . . she's the goddess of curves. And then there was me. Endowed with nothing, forced to stuff my bras with all kinds of paper products and ashamed to change in the locker room. I mean, I walk around, self-conscious about my body, watching people examine me as I pass by. I censor my wardrobe, only wearing shirts that are way too big .
. . nothing skin tight. And it's not like looking in the mirror boosts my confidence. I just am unpleased with the figure starring back at me. Guys barely glance my way and girls . . . girls are girls.

They dress up as adults in over-sized underwear, bras and panties of all sorts.

Men dream of winning women through combat. They fight a deadly fight in the manner of the calinda (stickfight). The women empty buckets of mud over their heads to stop this masculine ritual of combat. Loud scandalous laughter. Freeze.

6. TOWARDS ADULTHOOD

A VOICE

(To Audience as the devotees remain frozen in mud.)

The MUD INITIATION CEREMONY will now commence.

Here we have STRAWBERRY. She hails from Kansas and enjoys cigarettes. She is currently conducting STD research in her spare time.

Over in this corner we have BUTTERCUP from New Mexico. She is taking donations for her breast enlargement surgery.

Right here is PURPLE HAZE. He can still be seen in syndication on "Who Is The Boss?"

MUD!

> And over here we have HERCULES S an
> exotic penis pole dancer who has taken
> a keen interest recently in Devil
> Worship.

> OK. So now is the appropriate time to
> apply the latex gloves, the ones you
> received when you came in, to your
> hands. And use the mud provided to
> make these devotees into images of
> yourselves. Make your devotee resemble
> you as far as possible. When you are
> finished please dispose of the gloves in
> the appropriate receptacles to the left
> of your devotees.

*(After the audience/community members have
fully anointed the devotees. They are
encouraged to join in and paint their own
faces and arms as well. Everybody is painted
in mud, to some extent, by now. The devotees
remain frozen all through this mud-painting
process.)*

7. CELEBRATION TIME!

A VOICE

> And now, it is the time we have all
> waited for: LET THE CELEBRATIONS BEGIN!
> *(Music and chanting by everyone.)*

> We THE MUD PEOPLE of the OOZE celebrate
> This daybreak,

This ritual of becoming
This jouvay.
We here declare ourselves
In the morning of our lives
In this the dawn of our lives.
This is liberation time! Emancipation
time!
We declare ourselves!
(*Everyone dances a joyous dance of awakening,
of becoming.*)

8. JOUVAY - An Awakening

STRAWBERRY

(*Dressed as MISS AMERICA [BARBIE of the MUD]
Midnight Robber "Tombstone Gonorrhea" in red
spike-tailed shoes, a black plastic cape and
an apple in her hand.*)

Beware! Hot, Horny, American youth.
For I wait all week,
sometimes less, for you to open
your arms and your legs to me.
I am Gonorrhea,
and I crawl through the sweaty hoards
of you,
directing the solar system in a way
that brings you all together,
pelvis to pelvis,
and the three of us party all night
long.
I infect you without you even knowing
it.

MUD!

I may be stealth
but I conquer you all without breaking
a bead of sweat on my blistered face.

I was born on the darkest night
out of moonlight, incest, lust and
beer.
On the night I was born the moon
exploded
and all the women and the unborn babies
of the world cried out.
On my first day I killed a thousand
fetuses,
infecting them through their mother's
birth canals.
I ate half the mothers and left the
other half in the way of my honored
grandfather, HIV.
On my second day, I cast the most
powerful trance over all the men in the
world, directing them to follow their
penises wherever they go,
to ingest gallons of beer,
and to treat all the women of the world
as the booty buffet that they are.
I filled them with a potent aggression
and taught them to attack at the sight
of a tube top. I am the leader and the
enemy of my army, leading them to their
own demise
by dangling a wet, muddy, measly,
morsel of an orgasm before them.
Then I strike with the power of ten
thousand jack hammers, whisking the
bait of the orgasm away at the last

second.
I am Gonorrhea,
and I conquer you all without breaking
a bead of sweat on my blistered face.

*(PURPLE HAZE, who has been trying to
put a condom on his head all the while
approaches carrying a "little MUD
house" in one hand and an apple in the
other. He approaches STRAWBERRY and
offers her the house as a future. They
hold the house and dance together. A
dance of marriage. HERCULRS S, with
diabolic rage, bursts through them and
smashes the house. PURPLE HAZE, as a
FBI agent immediately tries to contain
him by catching him in a length of
rope around his waist. Throughout the
following speech HERCULES S is trying
to pull away from PURPLE HAZE in the
manner of the Blue Devil masquerade
dance.)*

HERCULES S

No. All your faces are unknown.
Actually, "unknown" is the wrong word…
.all your faces are very fresh…..fresh
and new. New, but definitely not
unfamiliar. (*Pause.*)
You must think I'm a crazy Muslim
fanatic. Must be still running
around trying to save yourselves from
the memories of that day. Must be
asking yourselves: Who is Mohammed
Atta? Why are innocent people dying

because of him? Some of you may know
me directly or might have met me, but
must be refusing the acquaintance after
September 11.
You know how old I am? I'm 33! Think
I'm lying because I look so young? The
mystery behind my youth is my death.
Ahhh yes, my death…. untimely, but
gratefully accepted.
I was born and raised in Kafr-El-
Sheik, a city on the Nile delta. I
remember being a shy young man. Quiet.
Skinny. Quite skinny. My father was a
lawyer and my mother was a homemaker.
Didn't really care much for religion
or politics. My two older sisters…
.now they were smart…..one became a
Zoology professor and the other became
a medical doctor. I received a degree
in architectural engineering from Cairo
University and in 1992, enrolled at
the Technical University of Hamburg in
northern Germany. So you see…..I'm not
some crazy, insane loafer. Quite the
ladies man…..wouldn't you agree?
But the interesting part of the
biography of Mohammed Atta starts now.
In a sense, I lived only for one day.
Oh, I almost forgot one small detail
about my life. I could never stand
injustice, big or small…even got
emotional when people killed insects.
As I grew older, I learned more about
the injustices of the world. I took
a keen interest in history, especially

Islamic history. The more I learned…
the more I realized that the United
States was the root of terrorism around
the world. I loved Islam, but also
saw how modernity was destroying its
ancient traditions. Allah, peace be
unto him, became the only Truth for me.
Yah Allah….the US had to be destroyed,
not for its people, but for it's
government's corrupt policies. So many
injustices……5,000 poor people killed
in Panama, 2 million in Vietnam, atomic
bombs killing civilians in Japan,
sanctions killing 500,000 children in
Iraq.

Yah Allah . . .
(*Chorus*) So many, so many!
Yah Allah . . .
(*Chorus*) So many, so many!
Yah Allah . . .
(*Chorus*) So many, so many!
Yah Allah . . .
(*Chorus*) So many, so many!
Yah Allah . . .
(*Chorus*) So many, so many!
Yah Allah . . .
(*Chorus*) So many, so many!

We had only one option—to destroy the
infidels who went against the word of
The Merciful. Peace be unto him. We
trained to be warriors. Those who died
were blessed as martyrs for a just
cause. If you observe carefully, we

     bombed symbols of America's economic
     and military dominance. Not the Statue
     of Liberty! We who gave our lives also
     believe in freedom and democracy!

     Yes, yes….there is definitely an
     emergency—9-1-1. Mother Earth is in
     need of help. You know something…I
     still think about it and it makes
     me laugh. Me….Mohammed Atta flying a
     fucking plane! I can hardly ride a
     bicycle. Courage allows one to do some
     amazing things….no? All you people
     live for your principles. The only
     difference is that I was prepared to
     die for my principles.

*All scream in an act of self-immolation,
inflicting physical pain with mud and lashing
of the body. This goes on for a while as
they search for lost ones in the war zone
wreckage. It gets louder and louder and more
and more intense. A deafening intensity.
Silence.*

*Suddenly PURPLE HAZE wrestles HERCULES S to
the ground and attempts to tie him up with
the rope.*

PURPLE HAZE

    You piece of shit you . . .

HERCULES S

Let go of me! Get off me! I am Sai, an

American citizen. You understand? An
American citizen.

PURPLE HAZE

What? But . . .

EVERYONE (*Repeat over and over.*)

I am an American citizen . . .
I am an American citizen . . .
I am an American citizen . . .
I am an American citizen . . .

STRAWBERRY

*Recites an excerpt from
W. H. Auden's SEPTEMBER 1ST, 1939*)

"All I have is a voice
To undo the folded lie,
The romantic lie in the brain
Of the sensual man-in-the-street
And the lie of Authority
Whose buildings grope the sky:
There is no such thing as the State
And no one exists alone;
Hunger allows no choice
To the citizen or the police;
We must love one another or die."

(*From ANOTHER TIME by W. H. Auden, Random
House, Copyright © 1940, renewed by The
Estate of W. H. Auden.*)

MUD!

9. THE EXIT - Epilogue

THE CAST

(Sings WOYAYA by Osibisa-AIM 1046CD ©1995)
    We are going
    Heaven knows where
    We are going
    We know within

    We will get there
    Heaven knows how
    We will get there
    We know we will

    It will be hard
    We know
   And the road will be muddy and rough

(Audience encouraged to join in.)
    But we'll get there
    Heaven knows how
    We will get there
    We know we will

Share with your community a meal of fresh, cooked or uncooked, vegetables and fruits to be washed down by freshly squeezed fruit juices.

FADE

END OF RITUAL

About The Author

Tony Hall is a playwright and moviemaker. In the theatre, he worked extensively in Western Canada with Catalyst Theatre and in the Caribbean with Derek Walcott's Trinidad Theatre Workshop and with Banyan Television. At Banyan he co-directed and appeared in AND THE DISH RAN AWAY WITH THE SPOON (1992) (US Release date: 1994) - An award winning Banyan Film for a BBC/TVE series. Tony founded, with Errol Fabien, Lordstreet Theatre Company with the prize winning jouvay mas trilogy of bands, A Band on Drugs (1991), A Band on Violence (1992) and A Band on US (1993). His plays include: The award winning JEAN & DINAH . . . (1994), successfully performed in the Caribbean, first performed in the US in 1998 at Trinity College's Goodwin Theater and in Canada at Artword Theatre, Toronto in 2001; also the acclaimed RED HOUSE *[Fire! Fire!]* premiered in 1999 and the controversial TWILIGHT CAFÉ (The Last Breakfast) was first performed in 2002. Mr. Hall has been Visiting Artist in Residence at Trinity College, Hartford, CT since 1998. He divides his time between Hartford and his home island of Tobago in the West Indies.